What the papers say about Vernon Coleman:

'No thinking person can ignore him.' THE ECOLOGIST

'The calmest voice of reason.' THE OBSERVER

'A godsend.' DAILY TELEGRAPH

'Superstar.' INDEPENDENT ON SUNDAY

'Brilliant!' THE PEOPLE

'Compulsive reading.' THE GUARDIAN

'His message is important.' THE ECONOMIST

'He's the Lone Ranger, Robin Hood and the Equalizer rolled into one.' GLASGOW EVENING TIMES

'The man is a national treasure.' WHAT DOCTORS DON'T TELL YOU

'His advice is optimistic and enthusiastic.' BMJ

'Revered guru of medicine.' NURSING TIMES

'Hard hitting…inimitably forthright.' HULL DAILY MAIL

'Refreshingly forthright.' LIVERPOOL DAILY POST

'It's impossible not to be impressed.' WESTERN DAILY PRESS

'Outspoken and alert.' SUNDAY EXPRESS

'Controversial and devastating.' PUBLISHING NEWS

'Dr Coleman made me think again.' BBC WORLD SERVICE

'Marvellously succinct, refreshingly sensible.' THE SPECTATOR

'Probably one of the most brilliant men alive today.' IRISH TIMES

'Vernon Coleman writes brilliant books.' THE GOOD BOOK GUIDE

Bloodless
Revolution

Books by Vernon Coleman include:

The Medicine Men (1975)
Paper Doctors (1976)
Stress Control (1978)
The Home Pharmacy (1980)
Aspirin or Ambulance (1980)
Face Values (1981)
The Good Medicine Guide (1982)
Bodypower (1983)
Thomas Winsden's Cricketing Almanack (1983)
Diary of a Cricket Lover (1984)
Bodysense (1984)
Life Without Tranquillisers (1985)
The Story Of Medicine (1985, 1998)
Mindpower (1986)
Addicts and Addictions (1986)
Dr Vernon Coleman's Guide To Alternative Medicine (1988)
Stress Management Techniques (1988)
Know Yourself (1988)
The Health Scandal (1988)
The 20 Minute Health Check (1989)
Sex For Everyone (1989)
Mind Over Body (1989)
Eat Green Lose Weight (1990)
How To Overcome Toxic Stress (1990)
Why Animal Experiments Must Stop (1991)
The Drugs Myth (1992)
Complete Guide To Sex (1993)
How to Conquer Backache (1993)
How to Conquer Pain (1993)
Betrayal of Trust (1994)
Know Your Drugs (1994, 1997)
Food for Thought (1994, revised edition 2000)
The Traditional Home Doctor (1994)
People Watching (1995)
Relief from IBS (1995)
The Parent's Handbook (1995)
Men in Dresses (1996)
Power over Cancer (1996)
Crossdressing (1996)

How to Conquer Arthritis (1996)
High Blood Pressure (1996)
How To Stop Your Doctor Killing You (1996, revised edition 2003)
Fighting For Animals (1996)
Alice and Other Friends (1996)
Spiritpower (1997)
How To Publish Your Own Book (1999)
How To Relax and Overcome Stress (1999)
Animal Rights – Human Wrongs (1999)
Superbody (1999)
Complete Guide to Life (2000)
Strange But True (2000)
Daily Inspirations (2000)
Stomach Problems: Relief At Last (2001)
How To Overcome Guilt (2001)
How To Live Longer (2001)
Sex (2001)
We Love Cats (2002)
England Our England (2002)
Rogue Nation (2003)
People Push Bottles Up Peaceniks (2003)
The Cats' Own Annual (2003)
Confronting The Global Bully (2004)
Saving England (2004)
Why Everything Is Going To Get Worse Before It Gets Better (2004)
The Secret Lives of Cats (2004)
The Cat Basket (2005)
The Truth They Won't Tell You (And Don't Want You To Know) About The EU (2005)
Living in a Fascist Country (2006)
How To Protect & Preserve Your Freedom, Identity & Privacy (2006)
The Cataholic's Handbook (2006)
Animal Experiments: Simple Truths (2006)
Coleman's Laws (2006)
Secrets of Paris (2007)
Cat Fables (2007)
Too Sexy To Print (2007)
Oil Apocalypse (2007)
Gordon is a Moron (2007)

The OFPIS File (2008)
Cat Tales (2008)
What Happens Next? (2009)
Moneypower (2009)

novels
The Village Cricket Tour (1990)
The Bilbury Chronicles (1992)
Bilbury Grange (1993)
Mrs Caldicot's Cabbage War (1993)
Bilbury Revels (1994)
Deadline (1994)
The Man Who Inherited a Golf Course (1995)
Bilbury Pie (1995)
Bilbury Country (1996)
Second Innings (1999)
Around the Wicket (2000)
It's Never Too Late (2001)
Paris In My Springtime (2002)
Mrs Caldicot's Knickerbocker Glory (2003)
Too Many Clubs And Not Enough Balls (2005)
Tunnel (1980, 2005)
Mr Henry Mulligan (2007)
Bilbury Village (2008)
Bilbury Pudding (2009)

as Edward Vernon
Practice Makes Perfect (1977)
Practise What You Preach (1978)
Getting Into Practice (1979)
Aphrodisiacs – An Owner's Manual (1983)

with Alice
Alice's Diary (1989)
Alice's Adventures (1992)

with Donna Antoinette Coleman
How To Conquer Health Problems Between Ages 50 & 120 (2003)
Health Secrets Doctors Share With Their Families (2005)
Animal Miscellany (2008)

Bloodless Revolution

How we can change the world in a day

Plus:
Two Dozen Life Changing Things We Can Do
(If We Want To) When We've Got Rid Of The
Political Parties

Vernon Coleman

BLUE
BOOKS

Published by Blue Books, Publishing House, Trinity Place, Barnstaple, Devon EX32 9HG, England.

ISBN: 978-1-899726-16-5

A catalogue record for this book is available from the British Library.

Printed by CPI Cox & Wyman

Dedication

To Donna Antoinette
When you fear I fear with you.
When you are sad I am sad with you.
When you rejoice I rejoice for you.
When there is sunshine we will share it together.
When there is tempest we will endure it together.
We have a thousand adventures ahead of us. We will greet them all together and so enjoy our triumphs and overcome our tribulations.

Contents List

Bloodless Revolution contains the answer to the eternal question: 'What can I do to change things?'

VERNON COLEMAN

Part One
Why We Need A Revolution (We're In A Terrible State)

1

Although this may come as an unpleasant surprise to those who believe that the fundamental aim of a government is to provide chauffeur-driven limousines and huge expense accounts for faithful supporters of the controlling party, the primary purpose of a proper democratic government is to protect the lives, liberty and property of its citizens. We don't so much need leaders (heaven knows, they are in short enough supply) as effective managers.

Nineteenth Century American writer William Leggett believed that a government's legislative activities should be restricted to the making of general laws, uniform and universal in their operation, for the sole purpose of protecting people and their property. Politicians should provide a simple, comprehensible code of laws telling citizens what they cannot do. Everything that is not illegal should be legal.

I would add to that only that it is also the government's job to provide armed forces, to ensure that we cannot easily be overwhelmed by an invading force, and to provide a judicial system capable of ensuring that the nation's laws are upheld and that the freedom of the citizens is protected.

Other than providing the armed forces (and embassies to represent the country abroad) it is difficult to see why the Government should stick its nose into any other area of public or private life.

2

In a real democracy, the voters elect the legislature which makes the rules. The executive runs things according to the rules. And the judiciary decides if rules have been broken. It's a simple system. But ours has broken down. Today's MPs are an irrelevance, ignored by the party leadership and forced to become voting lobby fodder; they are emasculated ghosts who know that in order to be rewarded with a ministerial car and chauffeur they must do what they are told. Mavericks are as rare as mares' nests. Career politicians leave university, work as 'advisers' in Westminster and then move directly into Parliament, and on into the cabinet, with little or no experience of the real world in which their constituents live. Moreover, 75% of new English legislation is made not by elected representatives but by unelected bureaucrats in Brussels.

The sad truth is that the modern MP has as much influence over modern legislation as has the dog next door.

3

The point of a social structure (a country, a city, a town or a village), and the purpose of electing people to take decisions (a government or a council and the bureaucratic paraphernalia of government), is to make our lives easier and safer.

The purpose of electing leaders (or nation managers) is to remove hazards, threats and burdens; to make it possible for citizens to walk, meet, play, shop, travel and go to work in the firm and honest belief that they will be able to do so safely and securely and with the minimum of fuss and inconvenience.

That's what Governments and councils are supposed to do.

It is not the job of those in Government (or sitting on a council) to acquire a huge self-serving infrastructure of their own, to accumulate power and authority for its own sake, or to line their pockets at the expense of the electorate.

4

Not all that long ago, when England ruled the world, she did so with a total complement of civil servants that would today be considered inadequate to administer a medium sized hospital or a small rural town. In the days of Queen Victoria, England's Home Office and Foreign Office ran the nation and the Empire for decades with no more than a handful of employees. Those employees worked for the benefit of the nation and the people.

Today, the Government, its many departments, and an ever-growing number of councils and public bodies, employ millions of people and are run largely for the convenience of those employees. The National Health Service, for example, is one of the largest employers in the world and the problems created within it are largely a result of the fact that the organisation is run not for the benefit of patients but for the benefit of the staff.

Modest sized local authorities throughout England now employ 20,000 to 30,000 people each. That's enough people to run an Empire. And all these people, working for the Government, for councils and for quangos, demand expensive services and perks. For example, the Home Office spends a million pounds a year of taxpayers' money on taxicabs. (That is, incidentally, a rise of £970,000 from the figure spent in 1997 when New Labour first came to power).

5

We need to ask some fundamental questions. And we need to find some real answers.

We need to decide precisely what we want the State to do. Do we want a multicultural nation? Do we approve of means-testing? Do we approve of political correctness? Do we want to be members of the European Union? How important is it that we retain our cultural and historical identity? Do we care about England and being English? Do we want our country to be run by politicians who start wars without our approval?

What do we want our politicians to do? Is there any role for political parties in managing the way our country is run? How much do we expect our elected representatives to control our day to day lives? How much power do we want to give away to the police and to foreign bureaucrats? How accountable should public servants be? Should those who do not work, and do not contribute to the State in any clear way, be allowed to continue controlling the way the State is managed (with the result that it is, in reality, managed and run for their benefit)? What aspects of our basic infrastructure should be run by the State? How should we choose our political representatives and who should vote for them?

These are fundamental questions.

No one ever asks them.

But now is the time.

And now is the time for us to find the answers.

You may be surprised to discover that, if we want change, if we want less government, lower taxes and more freedom, there is one incredibly simple way for us to change our world and obtain what we want.

I call it the bloodless revolution.

And this book explains how you can make a difference and take part in a bloodless revolution which will change England and restore our freedom and liberty. In order to take part in this revolution, you don't have to leave your home, spend any money or take any risks. Moreover, if enough of us take part the revolution is guaranteed to succeed. In one day. Individually it is difficult for any of us to make a difference. Together we can change the world.

That's the beauty of people power.

6

Our politicians claim that they want change and progress. But they don't really want major changes. They don't want innovative, imaginative structural changes of the kind I'm offering in this book.

We need to question everything which is regarded as 'normal', 'fixed' or 'necessary'.

Politicians merely want changes and progress which suit them.

7

The first purpose of this book is to offer some ideas which are never aired; some options and some possibilities which rarely, if ever, see the light of day.

We have to protect, preserve and defend the things which are important. But what is important? What are our priorities? When society is too structured (and becomes, as ours has, statist and fascist) we have to fight for a more open society. I deal with these issues in the second part of the book.

And the second purpose of this book (which I deal with first) is to explain how we can create a society in which those options can, if we wish, become reality.

With the political system we have at the moment, nothing will ever again be as good as it is today; we will never again have as much (or, as little) freedom as we have now.

If that doesn't terrify you, nothing will.

If we do nothing then things will get steadily worse and never better.

8

Our real enemies are not Muslim extremists (who hate us because of the actions of Blair and Brown but whose hatred is defined and particular) but our police, our bureaucrats, our politicians and, behind this pustulant pile, the fascist EU: the greatest threat to our freedom, and the mountainous obstacle in the path of our rescuing our lost and forgotten democracy.

The simple, basic, underlying reason for the problems we have is that we have given too much power to the political parties.

9

No government has a right to eavesdrop on its innocent citizens. And yet our government does this. We have no privacy. It has been taken from us in the name of protecting us.

In a free society every citizen has a fundamental right to say, write and publish whatever he or she wants to say, write or publish.

But, despite the existence of the Human Rights Act (and why do we need legislation to affirm our basic rights?) English citizens no longer enjoy this basic right. You and I can be arrested and imprisoned for saying, writing or publishing material of which the government does not approve.

10

Politics, like just about everything else in life, has been trivialised.

We are encouraged (by the media, and the politicians themselves) to concentrate on the minutiae. The big questions are never asked.

So, the fundamental political question: 'What is the purpose of the State?' is a question we have been encouraged to ignore.

And yet the answer to the question is remarkably simple.

The State's purpose is to provide services which could not properly be provided by individuals within communities. These requirements are more limited than they might now appear to be and the proper role of the State is considerably smaller than the role which politicians have adopted.

Any time a government does anything that isn't protecting the lives, liberty and property of its citizens it is failing in its duty or exceeding its authority.

The aim of all rulers, leaders and governments should be to secure and defend the fullest life possible for every citizen.

Nearly all rebellions in history are a result of rulers, leaders and governments failing to do this.

11

Our politicians live in a vacuum; isolated from honour, integrity and ideas; they are a product of circumstances rather than creators of circumstances; they are without dignity, imagination, honour or respect for themselves or anyone else. They are people with such a poorly developed sense of irony or decency that they will see nothing hypocritical in meeting to discuss world poverty and hunger and then enjoying together a sumptuous twelve course dinner.

12

In our politicians' hands England has become a barbarous nation, run by intellectual terrorists, philistines and thieves.

Our politicians have created a world in which those who are well-intentioned, honest or sensitive are seen as weak. Our politicians simply want us to obey, conform and consume.

In their hands, England has become a dirty country run by third rate administrators and uniformed bullies.

The politicians are running our lives with no regard for our rights and freedoms and no thought of what we, the people who pay for it all, might want.

13

There is, I believe, a simple reason for the mess our country is in, and the dramatic deterioration in the quality of our politicians.

That reason is the growth in the power of the major political parties.

Party politicians have damned nearly destroyed England. Politicians forget that they are elected not to govern us but to serve us. It is the party system which enables them to do this.

14

England is now grubby, shabby, down at heel. Our streets and motorways are littered with rubbish. Our railway stations and airports are packed with people being bullied by rude petty, bureaucrats (many of whom don't even speak English very well). The mass of people are depressed and have given up hope. Small and medium sized businesses, the backbone of the nation and its future too, are being strangled by red tape. Entrepreneurs struggling to build new businesses, the lifeblood of any society, are oppressed by absurd and unhelpful legislation and by a vast variety of taxes.

Never before have so many people led lives of such quiet desperation.

We have to move quickly.

The only way to get our country back, and to stop the politicians destroying it completely, is to get rid of the party political system which now serves us so badly, and to replace our system of government with a free, truly independent, parliamentary democracy.

15

Party politicians are determined to control every aspect of our lives. They need to do this in order to ensure that their party stays in power for as long as possible.

16

The party system which dominates our political processes gives complete authority over parliament to the party which wins an election. And authority is the veneer under which lies the constant, ever-increasing threat of violence.

The leader of the winning party runs the country, and hands out appointments and honours to his or her supporters. He or she has enormous, almost limitless, power.

Since campaigning is largely done by national parties, rather than by individuals with a genuine interest in representing a particular constituency, parliamentary seats are handed out to party supporters.

The result is that parliamentary elections are effectively conducted in secret, in party committee rooms, rather than via the ballot box.

In recent years this system has failed the nation for several reasons.

First, the traditional system of government by a cabinet of politicians has been replaced by a system more suitable to a totalitarian state or a dictatorship. A single politician pushes through his own plans with little or no regard for the wishes of the cabinet he has appointed. Parliament is virtually ignored. Since MPs are nearly all members of a party (and must, if they want to retain their seats, follow the party line on important issues) the leader of the biggest party controls Parliament.

Second, the needs of the party are given priority over the needs of the nation. Policies are adopted and pursued because they help satisfy the short, medium and long-term needs of the party. The leader of the party knows that his authority depends upon his protecting and strengthening the party he represents.

17

The consequences of the financial crash of 2007 and 2008 (and onwards) may be England's biggest problem for the second decade of the 21st Century. But the four things which have destroyed the very fabric of our country (and which will make it more difficult for us to recover) are multiculturalism, political-correctness, means-testing and the insistence on public bodies meeting artificial targets.

The sole real purpose of a government is to provide an infrastructure designed to enable citizens to go about their business safely and freely.

Instead, for ten years, we have had a government committed to social engineering. And for several generations we have had governments which have (for a variety of largely secret reasons) been subservient to a foreign power – the European Union.

18

The Labour Party's decisions to ignore their own promise to have a referendum before signing the Lisbon Treaty signalled the end of democracy in England, and confirmed that England had become a fascist region within a fascist state.

Constitutional experts concluded that it was against the law for the Government not to provide a referendum (whether one had been promised or not) but the Labour Government doesn't much care about the law, the people or democracy.

19

Despite the rapid growth in the number of civil servants employed in England, the people who really run England now are bureaucrats in Brussels, bankers in the USA and businessmen in countries as far apart as France, India and China.

Thanks to our political parties, big decisions are made not by local people but by nameless, faceless bureaucrats and by distant politicians and businessmen

20

Even small decisions are no longer made locally.

For example, the Labour Government recently told council planners that: 'the sheer scale of public protest or opposition to a planning proposal should not be regarded as a factor when considering a planning application'.

And so, local planning officers now ignore protests from local people and make decisions pretty much as they please. Power has been transferred from the people to the bureaucrats.

Local people can protest and hold meetings and even decide unanimously that they are opposed to a development of some kind, but their wishes will be ignored. The development will be approved by a politician or a bureaucrat who has never been within a hundred miles of the area and who knows nothing of the locality's needs.

Central Government politicians and bureaucrats make decisions and overrule local councils whenever they want to.

21

Our politicians are carefully and deliberately taking away every last vestige of our privacy. They are, they claim, doing this so that they can protect us. (Only those who believe in the tooth fairy believe this.)

Several years ago I pointed out that the new identity (ID) cards being introduced by the Government would make our confidential information available to just about anyone who wanted to see it. It is now clear that my warning was justified. The information on the ID cards we will all be forced to buy (and carry at all times) will be available to around 44,000 organisations. Government departments (such as the taxman) and private companies (such as banks and mobile phone companies) will be able to see all the information you thought was confidential. Nothing about you will be private. And you will have to produce your ID card to make any purchase, to travel or to leave your home. (The Government, desperate to save money and win votes, has announced that the ID card scheme will be voluntary. But the EU wants compulsory ID cards. And the EU is in charge, not the Government.)

On the other hand, the Government is quick enough to worry about its own privacy.

When the Government refused to release the minutes from the Cabinet's meetings about whether or not to invade Iraq, a Labour Party politician, Jack Straw, vetoed their release on the grounds that releasing the information would do serious damage to the Cabinet. (No mention was made of the need to publish the truth, or of the public's right to know, or of the fact that the decision to go to war had been taken in our name and had exposed citizens to great danger.)

When a photographer took a picture of Scotland Yard's assistant commissioner carrying top-secret counter-terrorism documents, politicians called not for policemen to carry their confidential documents in briefcases but for tighter restrictions on photographers. (There are already pretty strict restrictions in existence. According to the counter-Terrorism Act 2008, it is against the law to publish information about the intelligence services that is likely to be useful to a person committing or preparing an act of terrorism. And so, it is against the law to take photographs of policemen beating up innocent members of the public. The police are, of course, allowed to film and photograph innocent protestors.)

There are closed circuit television (CCTV) cameras absolutely everywhere in England (more than anywhere else in the world) but, oddly enough, whenever footage might embarrass the authorities there is a problem; the relevant footage is accidentally erased, or the camera was facing the wrong way or the film wasn't clear enough or there was marmalade in the equipment.

22

'Why should government agents spy on us?' asked Judge Andrew Napolitano, in the USA. 'They work for us. How about we spy on them. On cops when they arrest and interrogate people or contemplate suspending freedom; on prosecutors when they decide whom to prosecute and what evidence to use; on judges when they rationalise away our guaranteed rights; and on members of Congress whenever they meet with a lobbyist, mark up a piece of legislation, or conspire to assault our liberties or our pocket books.'

Bravo.

23

At least a quarter of all Government databases are illegal. These intrusive collections of private information cost billions of pounds of taxpayers' money and are in clear breach of human rights law. The Government simply ignores the law when it seems convenient or profitable to do so.

24

We have more public servants than ever before. And yet our public services are worse than they were a hundred years ago. This is no curious coincidence. I take a close interest in politics but I have to confess that I am constantly finding Government departments I've never heard of, and ministerial posts I didn't know existed.

We are also learning (as if we needed to) that huge bureaucracies, with centralised power, reduce individual freedom. Democracy only survives when there is a small national bureaucracy and small local bureaucracies.

25

The majority of our civil servants are, as the old joke has it, neither civil nor servile. On the contrary our public sector workers are, as a breed, lazy, greedy, smug, humourless (try cracking a joke to one), arrogant, heavy-handed and overpaid.

They work very few hours, take more holidays than private

BLOODLESS REVOLUTION

sector workers, are paid better than private sector workers and have massive pensions (paid by taxpayers). They have job security and virtually unlimited days off work when they are feeling a little under the weather.

They are treated in ways that private sector workers could only dream of. For example, I know of one who became ill. Her local authority employer converted the office entrance (at huge public expense) so that she could continue to attend work. After a couple of weeks she announced that she would in future prefer to work from home. The local authority then spent a fortune converting her home so that she could work from home. She then decided that she would retire.

26

Civil servants are hardly ever disciplined (whatever terrible mistakes they make) and hardly ever fired (if they are, or if they choose to resign, they are often given a huge tax-free pay-off to smooth their way into the real world). They are given massive holidays (more than six weeks a year is quite normal).

And they are given the sort of bonuses which were, in the very early years of the 21st Century, given to the greediest, most overpaid and most incompetent bankers.

Indeed, bonuses have become as fashionable as scented candles. There isn't even any pretence that bonuses are given for success or for hard work above and beyond the requirements of the job. Among bankers and civil servants and politicians there is an exaggerated sense of entitlement. Too many of these people seem to believe that they deserve to get rich solely because of the position they occupy, rather than because they have talent or because they work hard.

Civil servants above the rank of lollipop manipulator used to be content with a knighthood at the age of 55. Now they expect a knighthood and a quarter of a million quid in hard cash as an annual reward for being kind enough to do their jobs.

Civil servants are frequently given bonuses just for turning up and deigning to do what they are paid to do. If you think I'm exaggerating, read on.

After it snowed in London in February 2009, public employees working at the Crown Prosecution Service were given £250 bonuses for actually taking the trouble to turn up for work.

How many private companies could afford to give bonuses to employees who bothered to turn up for work?

Bonuses are often given as a reward for abject failure. After the credit crunch, employees at the Financial Services Authority (one of Gordon the Moron's mad inventions, and widely regarded as one of the main reasons for the country being in a mess) were smothered in bonuses.

'You did an appalling job so here's a wheelbarrow full of taxpayers' money to cheer you up!'

27

The civil service has been politicised. Civil servants no longer provide independent protection for the public. Instead, they work to preserve the power of the politicians and, thereby, of the State and the party which is in power.

The code for civil servants rules that they should act with integrity and honesty and that they should do their work objectively and impartially.

There are, almost certainly, some civil servants who take these rules seriously and who still struggle to satisfy them.

But, sadly, in today's huge sprawling bureaucracies there are many who don't, and who give their loyalty and allegiance to politicians or to commercial contacts rather than to electors.

And you only need a few bad eggs in a department for the work of that department to be defiled. The integrity of a department is as good as the integrity of the most dishonest person working there. Today, there isn't a single Ministry which obeys the civil service code en masse and is, in modern parlance, fit for purpose.

Today, the inglorious State is run by self-glorying, self-serving, morally delinquent politicians who were hired to protect individual citizens but who have adopted policies designed to exploit the citizens and to take advantage of them.

28

Tony Blair and Gordon Brown, the two politicians who took England to the end of the 20th Century, led it into the beginning of the 21st Century and, in my view, did more damage to the nation than any other pair of villains in history, both claim to have religious beliefs but both appear to me to have steadfastly ignored basic moral guidelines.

In my book *Rogue Nation* I argued that Tony Blair led Britain to war against Iraq not because he believed that the Iraqis had weapons of mass destruction hidden in the sand, not to save the Iraqi people from a tyrant (he didn't bother to invade Zimbabwe) and not to help the Americans grab the oil in Iraq, but so that he would be enriched by American businessmen (and, in particular, by Jewish American businessmen) when he left politics.

Well, just in case you missed it, Blair is now a very rich man. He receives £2 million a year from American bank JP Morgan Chase, and has received fees of $250,000 for a 45 minute speech on the American lecture circuit. He was given a $1 million prize for his 'determination to forge lasting solutions in conflict areas' by the Dan David Foundation of Tel Aviv. (Since Blair was, at the time, also being paid as a 'peacekeeping envoy', supposedly to broker peace between the Israelis and the Palestinians, accepting this generous prize seemed to me slightly tactless to say the least).

And in March 2009 it was revealed that Blair was setting up a company advising world leaders on 'good governance' (starting with a £1 million deal from Kuwait, where the men with the chequebooks obviously have a more developed sense of humour than I had suspected.). Naturally, Blair also receives a huge pension from the taxpayers (£63,348 the last time I looked).

Brown, forever boasting of his pride in being the son of the manse, said nothing in opposition to Blair's wars, presumably lest he damage his own self-serving ambitions. Brown, like Sir Thomas More, seems capable of promoting great ideals in principle but capable of doing or endorsing terrible things in practice.

29

Honest leaders create an environment, and circumstances, in which justice thrives and then they lead by example. (Why does everyone sneer at the idea of people setting a good example?)

We have, time and time again, been betrayed.

We expect our leaders to show self-restraint and to show us respect.

We have, time and time again, been disappointed.

It is a love of justice, rather than riches, that stirs the average Englishman to action. And nothing arouses an Englishman more than injustice.

30 .

The aim of politicians today is to keep their party in power for as long as possible. The longer the party is kept in power, and the stronger it becomes, the longer they will stay in power and the richer they will become.

If there were no political parties, independent MPs would be able to remain in Parliament merely by representing their constituents honestly and honourably. Without a political party to defend and to protect, individual MPs would be rewarded by the voters for showing their independence and their honesty because their loyalty and allegiance would be to their local electorate and not to a political party.

31

Today, the Government is the biggest source of terrorism in our lives. We are overwhelmed by the terrorism of State control. Our traditional values have been replaced with oppressive laws allegedly designed to protect us from violence but in practice designed to impose a reign of terror similar to that which followed the French Revolution. We have become a police state.

32

Whether or not the threat of terrorist attacks really increases one thing is for certain: the threat will continue to be used as an excuse for increasingly oppressive legislation. The Government has made Britain the world's number two target for militant Muslims (and much easier to hit than the USA because of Britain's open door immigration policies).

33

It is sometimes argued by politicians who want to defend England's oppressive regime that those who attack us are inspired by a hatred of anything western and that they will bomb us whatever we do.

This is, to put it politely, a barefaced lie.

Iran's Ayatollah Khomeneini tried for a decade to instigate an anti-Western jihad. It failed miserably. Muslims do not become suicide bombers because they dislike our lifestyle or religious beliefs. And they do not become suicide bombers because they are attracted by the prospect of instant entry into paradise. They do, however, become suicide bombers when we attack Muslim countries (or support those who do). Robert Pape, of the University of Chicago collected details of 462 suicide terrorist attacks which took place in the years after 1980 for his book *Dying to Win: The Strategic Logic Of Suicide Terrorism*. He found that the strongest motivation is not religion but a desire 'to compel modern democracies to withdraw military forces from the territory the terrorists view as their homeland'.

There were 41 suicide terrorist attacks in Lebanon between 1982 and 1986. When the USA, France and Israel withdrew their forces from Lebanon the suicide bomber attacks stopped completely.

Before Bush and Blair invaded Iraq in 2003, Iraq had never had a suicide terrorist attack in its entire history. Those who supported the invasions of Iraq and Afghanistan have made Britain a long-term target for terror attacks that will continue until our army leaves those countries.

It wasn't difficult to see this coming. When Blair first took us into the Iraq war I warned that his self-serving actions would result in Britons becoming a terrorist target.

The Blairs of this world don't seem to have the sensitivity or intelligence to realise this but when you bomb people who haven't done anything to hurt you, impose sanctions, support police states and steal their nation's natural resources there is a chance that they will be upset and want to strike back.

Speaking on American television, Bill Clinton's secretary of state, Madeleine Albright, said that the half a million Iraqi children who had died as a result of the sanctions on Iraq during the 1990s were 'worth it'.

How would the Americans like it if a foreign leader said that killing half a million American children in order to steal American oil was 'worth it'?

34

The Labour Government's uncritical support for America's imperialist policies has put us in great danger and made us far more vulnerable than we might otherwise have been. (The Secret Intelligence Service even has a word for what has happened. They use the word 'blowback', which, in these circumstances, is defined as 'the unintended consequences of military intervention'. I have no doubt that if the House of Commons had consisted of independent members of parliament the Government would not have been able to start its illegal wars in Iraq and Afghanistan.

35

Party politicians need to keep control of the electorate in order to keep control of the power.

The political party which is in office has all the power and all the money. Other MPs, representing the other parties are virtually pointless; the people they represent are effectively disenfranchised for the period of the parliament.

And, because the best way to control a population is through fear, the Government has deliberately created fear among the people. Life has become a continuing, never ending, series of threats.

In addition, the Government has used its anti-terror legislation to control dissent of any kind. Today, any demonstration or protest will be subject to anti-terrorism legislation. If a group of mothers protest about a dangerous roadway near to a school the fact that they are protesting will mean that they can be treated as terrorists.

Since 1997, governments run by a single political party have introduced a mass of legislation which no democratic parliament, consisting of independent MPs, could possibly have approved. The party system gives the leaders of political parties enormous power, and effectively turns them into dictators for the duration of their parliament.

Many of our new laws are deliberately ambiguous. New laws are added to old ones (laws are very rarely repealed). We assume that things have to be this way because, well, that's the way they are. Much of the anti-terrorism legislation introduced within the last decade leaves much to the judgement of individual police officers. As a result it has become impossible for protestors to know what they can and cannot do. No properly democratic parliament, full of independent MPs, would have ever given the police such wide-ranging and oppressive powers.

36

When a man who was accused of assaulting a policeman was arrested he was refused access to the CCTV cameras which showed the assault. He was shown the pictures only when he appeared in court. The defendant told the court that a passer-by had also filmed the incident on a mobile telephone. But those pictures did not exist. The police had demanded the telephone and had deleted the pictures.

According to one Justice of the Peace: 'it seems it is normal Metropolitan Police practice to seize mobile phones in order to delete pictures involving them' (the police).

So, it seems that the police are now deliberately destroying evidence and withholding evidence from accused citizens.

37

Every time there is a demonstration the police are widely, and justifiably, criticised for their heavy handedness and brutality. In other countries it has been shown that it is safer and more effective to manage large crowds using officers in ordinary uniform. (This has, for example, been done effectively in Northern Ireland.) But in England the police who attend public demonstrations are dressed in full riot gear and frequently take advantage of their absurdly wide powers.

38

The police seem to see it as their role to disrupt protests (and encourage future protesters to stay at home) rather than to make sure that neither people nor property are damaged.

When there is violence it is invariably the police who start the trouble. Policemen, protected by helmets, flak jackets and shields, seem to be enjoying themselves as they wield their official issue weapons.

The Labour Government has introduced a whole armoury of legislation designed to give the police new powers to ban or control demonstrations.

39

Police brutality at demonstrations has become commonplace. Policemen who cover up their faces and numbers when attending demonstrations are clearly planning to break the law.

But it isn't just ordinary policemen who are at fault. Police bosses lie, lie and lie again. Evidence disappears. Time and time again, the police beat people up, shoot them, run them over and then suppress or distort the truth about what they have done.

The police are out of control and have, quite rightly, lost our trust. No honest parliament of independent men and women would have allowed this to happen. The police could only acquire such outrageous power (and behave so badly) in a nation run by and (more importantly) for a political party.

40

The party politicians have filled our lives with meaningless detail and (literally) hundreds of thousands of new rules and regulations. If you want to do this then you must first do this and this and this and then pay this and then we will perhaps think about letting you do what you want to do. Maybe. We used to have lists of things we couldn't do. But now there are lists of things we can do if we pay the requisite fee, fill in the proper form, produce the appropriate paperwork and grovel to the right low-level bureaucrats.

41

Under Labour the rich have got richer and the poor have got poorer. The incidence of iatrogenesis (doctor-induced disease) has soared (and is now endemic in the National Health Service). The incidence of illiteracy has become so widespread as to be unworthy of note.

Hard work, thrift and prudence have been denigrated while theft and cheating have been rewarded at every level.

Having introduced and strengthened a system which encourages laziness and fraud, politicians have tried to deal with the sickness they have created by encouraging citizens to spy on one another (knowing that this creates distrust and fear).

If Blair, Brown et al had planned to destroy England they could not have made a better job of it.

Makes you wonder, doesn't it?

42

Rules and regulations (as many and as complicated as possible) are a good way to oppress a population. Today, millions are so worn out by regulations and pettiness that their vision, hope, ambition, aspirations, intuition, inspiration and ability to see the bigger picture (or think outside the box) have all disappeared.

If England were ruled by a parliament of independent MPs most of these rules and regulations would not exist.

43

We go through life hoping that if we do this or that then everything will eventually be all right and our path through life will be smoothed.

But our Government, instead of doing everything it can to make life easier for us, does the opposite. By making life more difficult, more full of fear and uncertainty, more unnerving, politicians know that they can prevent our finding the energy, or even the time, to rise up and protest, to defend ourselves and our country and to fight to retain our disappearing freedom and dignity.

Party politicians have to keep their party in power. They oppress us in order to control us.

Trusting and gullible, we believe them when they tell us it is necessary and in our interests. We believe them because we have to trust someone, because we don't believe anyone can lie that much and because we are frightened and don't believe we can make a difference anyway.

44

Professor Milton Friedman, the celebrated economist, once defined a liberal (defined elsewhere as someone who is happy to see governments liberally spend other people's money) as an individual who believes that all past laws were bad, but is convinced that all future laws will be good.

This is a triumph of hope over reality.

Similarly, party politicians and regulators believe that we need lots of new regulations because although all past regulations are bad (which is why we need the new stuff) all new regulations will be good.

Another triumph of hope over reality.

Party politicians love laws and regulations. They can never make enough of them. Laws and regulations give them and their party control.

45

Since 1997, the Labour Government has introduced, on average, one new criminal offence for every day they have been in power. Not even Hitler or Stalin managed so much oppressive legislation. There are twice as many things for which you can be put in prison as there were in 1997 when Tony Blair entered Downing Street on a carefully stage-managed wave of glory. The Labour Government has given itself the same powers which Hitler gave himself. (Many of these modern powers originated with the European Union – Hitler's dream.)

The Labour Government and Hitler used the same excuse for introducing new laws: the threat of terrorism.

It is now known that Hitler faked the threat.

46

Publicly expressed opinions can now be against the law. Saying (or writing) the wrong thing can result in a trial and imprisonment.

That's fascism.

Trying to decide what might or might not be illegal can itself be illegal.

People can be, and are, arrested and put in prison for things they only think of doing. Or are foolish enough to talk about.

By keeping low company (Straw, Blunkett, Reid, Smith et al) the law itself has been dragged into disrepute and downright contempt.

47

Lenin wrote that 'The purpose of terrorism is to terrorise'.

My dictionary defines terrorism as the 'unauthorised use of violence and intimidation in the pursuit of political aims'.

There is no doubt whatever that everything done by the Government and the European Union is done in the pursuit of political aims.

Did you authorise them to use violence and intimidation in the pursuit of their political aims?

If you did not, then they are, by definition, terrorists.

48

The Government has destroyed the economy by introducing complicated new taxes and miles of red tape, and by encouraging public sector expenditure paid for by a housing price bubble. They dramatically expanded the public sector payroll in order to help their party receive more votes. They have ignored their promises and handed over power to the European Union. They have deliberately made us targets by involving us in immoral and illegal wars.

The party politicians did all this in order to protect the interests of their party.

England is now not a democracy. It has become a fascist country, run by unelected, foreign bureaucrats.

With our nation's wealth and history it would have been so easy to have created a wonderful society: fair, just, healthy and well-educated, with well-planned towns and little crime.

But everything has been done with the aim of self-glorification, enrichment and, most of all, the survival of the party.

Bad motives inevitably lead to bad government.

49

Today the State controls *almost* everything. Politicians are not satisfied. They want to control everything.

We live in a world dominated and controlled by greedy, dishonest, ruthless, selfish, immoral people who care nothing for the public good but care only for using the system to their own financial advantage. Those who 'lead' us have sold out our past, present and future, and our peace, for party political advantage and for personal gain.

Our country has been run (and ruined) by a seemingly endless parade of incompetent and sometimes criminal people.

All markets are a conspiracy of insiders against outsiders but our Government, and the civil service we hire to do the paperwork, have together become a conspiracy of insiders.

A greedy few have always enriched themselves at the cost of the innocent many. In the past the greedy few were confidence tricksters who sometimes ended up in prison. Today the greedy few are politicians and bankers who end up on yachts and in the House of Lords.

50

'Efficient production will have little ultimate value, even in promoting human happiness, if it be accompanied by inefficient and vulgar consumption. In a true scale of values, liberty, security and reasonable leisure stand far higher than mere luxury.'

HARRY ROBERTS

51

Government ministers have repeatedly said that we must all share the responsibility for the mess the country is in. 'It is,' they say, 'our overspending and our greed which has put us all into this mess.'

This is unfair.

It was the greed of a minority which has caused the problem.

Politicians and journalists talk as though we were all to blame for the credit crunch. 'We were to blame,' they say, 'because we borrowed too much, bought things we couldn't afford and enjoyed a lifestyle which was (or should have been) beyond our reach.'

This is not a fair accusation.

Many people (particularly politicians) were greedy.

But many people were not greedy, and did not live beyond their means.

And yet the Government devised policies which were designed to help the greedy by punishing the prudent.

Why did they do this?

They did it because it was the expedient, self-serving thing to do. And because the prudent, being also self-effacing, let them get away with it. And because they themselves are greedy (and, therefore, have more sympathy with the greedy). And because the greedy make up a solid, selfish cadre of voters who can keep a party in power.

They did it to help preserve the power of the party.

52

We think we live in a free, capitalist society. We don't. It is now clear that we live in a state-directed version of capitalism. And what is that?

It's fascism.

Benito Mussolini (who knew of what he spoke because he invented practical fascism) said that 'fascism should more properly be called corporatism because it is the merger of state and corporate power'.

Fascism means putting society's needs above the individual's needs. Fascism means giving society rights which are greater than the rights of the individual. A State can be described as fascist when the needs and well-being of the State are put above the needs and well-being of the individual.

Our country has become fascist gradually and without most people noticing. But it has happened. As with totalitarianism we have a form of government in which all aspects of citizens' lives are subordinated to the authority of the State. All political institutions, and all old legal and social traditions, are being gradually replaced with new ones designed to meet the State's needs. The police increasingly operate without the constraint of laws and regulations.

53

Academics could debate for months about whether we live in a fascist country or a totalitarian one. Does it really matter? We certainly don't live in a democracy.

We live, let us not forget, in a regime which represses its own citizens and allows (even encourages) those in authority to abuse their power. Authority has been separated from responsibility and those who wield power seem to regard their posts primarily as routes to personal enrichment.

54

Here's a quick 'fascism' test, designed to help decide whether a nation is fascist. I've left the answers blank, so that you can fill them in yourself.

Question 1: Are honest, innocent law abiding citizens who attend demonstrations likely to be filmed and arrested?
Answer:

Question 2: Does the Government have the right to throw people into prison for weeks at a time without taking them to court?
Answer:

Question 3: Does the Government allow its citizens and/or its prisoners to be tortured in order to obtain information?
Answer:

Question 4: Does the Government routinely tap the telephones of innocent citizens?
Answer:

Question 5: Does the Government have (or plan to have) an Identity Card system? And will citizens be subject to arrest if they leave their homes without their ID cards? Will Government departments be entitled to access the 'confidential' information on the cards?
Answer:

Question 6: Has the Government installed CCTV cameras and satellite tracking equipment so that it can keep track of citizens' movements?
Answer:

Question 7: Is the Government collecting a national DNA database?
Answer:

Question 8: Does the Government take every opportunity to frighten its citizens by exaggerating threats?
Answer:

Question 9: Does the Government routinely ignore the will of the people, but put the needs of the State above everything else?
Answer:

Question 10: Does the Government control a large, publicly funded media organisation which provides the public with so-called 'news'? (And have independent observers shown that the media organisation is biased in favour of the State?)
Answer:

Question 11: Does the Government routinely distort statistics in order to hide the truth?
Answer:

Question 12: Does the Government plan to take fingerprints from all its citizens?
Answer:

Question 13: Does the Government control all serious opposition to the State philosophy (on whatever subject) by describing those who oppose its views or actions as terrorists - even though they may be entirely peaceful?
Answer:

Question 14: Does the Government do everything it can to prevent citizens expressing their right to free speech? (Remembering that freedom of speech means protecting the individual's right to say offensive or disturbing things. The right to say nice things needs no protection.)
Answer:

Question 15: Does the government try to suppress political parties which have views of which it does not approve?

Answer:

The more times you answered 'yes' the more likely it is that you are living in a fascist country.

55

So, we're living in a fascist country.

No argument.

The Government and the EU disagree, of course. They say that anyone who opposes them is a fascist.

That's what fascists always do.

56

Fascism can creep up on you slowly, like old age. Most people in England are unaware that it has happened for several reasons.

First, they don't really know what fascism is and so, not surprisingly, they have difficulty in recognising it.

Second, the fascists call everyone who opposes them a fascist. This is a double-edged weapon. It draws attention to the alleged fascist and takes attention away from the real fascist. It's an old trick but it still works. For example, supporters of the EU (without a doubt the most fascist organisation in the world today and, quite possibly the most successful fascist organisation ever to have existed) always demonise their critics by calling them fascists. If you aren't a europhile, they argue, then you must be a fascist.

57

It's vital to remember that although some of our fascism is home grown, most of it comes as a direct result of EU policies. England, Scotland and Wales have become statist sub units of the EU. All three major political parties in England are dedicated to supporting and promoting the European Union. All three major political parties in England are, therefore, fascist parties.

58

England now has over 100,000 laws which have come from the EU. All these have been added to the thousands of laws we had before.

Three quarters of our new legislation is made by unelected bureaucrats in Brussels and rubber stamped by overpaid, self-indulgent MPs in London.

59

Today, it is impossible even for lawyers and judges to know all the laws and so we are all at risk of inadvertently breaking one or more laws every day of our lives. Just getting through the day without being caught is, for many, quite a task.

Even specialist lawyers have confirmed to me that they cannot keep up with the new laws being introduced in their own specialist area of the law.

60

The EU, the world's most fascist organisation, is riddled with corruption and manned (and womanned) by thousands of overpaid incompetents. The EU, like the Nazis, believes in exhortations, threats, commands, demands and proclamations. What's the difference between Germany under the Nazis and Europe under the European Union?

Simple.

People voted for the Nazis. No one voted for the EU. The EU thrust itself upon us, stripped us, raped us and now holds us prisoner.

61

Our educational system, and the State broadcasting system (the Biased Broadcasting Corporation) are used to indoctrinate children into believing that the EU is a good, wholesome organisation with our best interests at heart.

The evidence proves that it is none of these things.

62

The existence of the EU makes border controls utterly pointless since millions of people from eastern Europe can now enter England legally, stay here legally and claim benefits legally.

63

Most Britons with functioning brain cells now recognise that staying in the EU means handing over all our power to a vast army of extraordinarily overpaid, faceless, nameless grey-suited bureaucrats living and working in a foreign country.

Staying in the EU also means giving most of our money to the same small army of bureaucrats so that they can give chunks of it to greedy and incompetent French farmers while lining their own nests with the rest.

British voters have had enough. Even the ones who were ill-informed enough to vote to join the Common Market in the first place now recognise that they made a mistake and want to put things right before it's too late.

But all three main British political parties are committed to keeping England in the EU. Political parties which are out of power may make noises about cutting the EU's power. But as soon as they get into power they quickly forget their promises and toe the EU line.

64

'The European Union ...is a German racket designed to take over the whole of Europe. It has to be thwarted...You might as well give it (sovereignty) to Adolf Hitler, frankly.'
NICHOLAS RIDLEY MP

65

All around the world, countries are getting smaller. Ethnic groups are fighting for their independence. Look at a map of Europe five years ago and you'll hardly recognise it.

Even within the United Kingdom there are those who are fighting for Home Rule for their part of the island.

Huge international conglomerates are shrinking, splitting up, demerging and 'downsizing' their global operations as it becomes increasingly clear that there are no advantages to being big – but that there are lots of advantages to being small.

But English electors now face the sort of situation which used to be the prerogative of Soviet voters in the old, one party communist days. We all have a vote. But there isn't a lot of choice involved.

The big issue for the future concerns the EU. Do we stay or do we go?

Voters can either choose to vote for a party that wants us to stay in Europe or they can choose not to vote. All the big political parties want to keep us in the EU.

That's the only choice.

And they call it freedom of choice.

66

So why are British politicians ignoring the wishes of the electors when they must surely know that if *their* party announced that it was planning to take us out of the European Union it would win by a landslide?

There's a simple answer.

First, the European Union is planning a one party State.

And that's a politician's dream.

Elections without the possibility of losing.

Second, politicians who support the European Union have a tendency to be well-rewarded.

Kinnock.

Mandelson.

Politicians are keen on a united Europe because they are driven by personal ambition. They don't want a bigger, stronger Europe because a bigger, stronger Europe will be good for the voters. They want a bigger, stronger Europe because it will be good for them.

67

Why do the three main parties in Britain all support the EU? Why do politicians refuse to criticise the EU or, even, to blame it when they are forced to implement unpopular legislation? (Most of the laws we hate originated in Brussels. But politicians still take the blame for the unpopular laws.)

Not since 1983 has a major political party in the UK talked openly about leaving the EU. Why do politicians ignore the will of the people?

I am always unwilling to accept conspiracy theories. But, as Sherlock Holmes pointed out, when you have excluded all other possibilities then whatever you have left, however impossible it may appear to be, must be the only realistic solution.

The only possible explanation is that the three main political parties in Britain are controlled by, and in thrall to, the European Union.

How could that be?

The answers aren't difficult to find.

First, politicians don't blame the EU for anything because they aren't allowed to. In 1971 the Foreign Office published a document entitled FCO 30/1048. In paragraph 24 the Foreign Office states: 'there would be a major responsibility on HMG and on all political parties not to exacerbate public concern by attributing unpopular measures or unfavourable economic developments to the remote and unmanageable workings of the Community.'

The Community is, of course, now known as the European Union. Whenever you see politicians struggling to defend a blatantly absurd policy or new piece of legislation you can rely on the fact that although the new policy or legislation is introduced and defended by British politicians it is the work of bureaucrats working in Brussels.

And second, our dishonest politicians are bribed to support the EU. There aren't many influential British politicians alive who have not at some stage in their careers received something from the European Union.

Money has always explained the link between politicians and

the EU. Edward Heath received a substantial financial reward for taking Britain into the EU when he was Prime Minister. The reward of £35,000, paid personally to Heath, in the guise of The Charlemagne Prize, was handed over to him after he had signed the Treaty of Rome. Heath later confirmed that he had lied to the British people about the implications of the Treaty. He told the electorate that signing the Treaty of Rome would lead to no essential loss of National Sovereignty but later admitted that this was a lie. He said he lied because he knew that the British would not approve of him signing the Treaty if they knew the truth.

Was Heath any worse than any other MP of modern times? I don't think so.

How much bribery currently goes on within the EU? That, of course, is impossible to say with precision. Bribery is, by its very nature, a secretive business. Neither those doing the bribing nor those being bribed are likely to talk much about what they are doing.

68

Peter Mandelson, like other politicians who have worked for the EU, is not allowed to criticise the European Union if he wants to keep hold of his pension as a former European Commissioner. (He receives his pension for having served as trade commissioner for just under four years.)

So, there's one Minister who may not stand up for our interests if there is a dispute with the EU.

A spokesman said that Mandelson did not see a contradiction between British patriotism and EU loyalty.

I bet he doesn't.

69

On behalf of the European Union, the Government is doing its best to remove England (and English history) from our minds.

English history isn't taught in much detail in schools these days. Indeed, when students are taught about English history at all (and, in particular, taught about English political history) they are given a bowdlerised, sanitised, politically correct version.

Modern students are taught that Big Government protects citizens from the wickedness of the free market. Students are taught to be ashamed of England's history; they are taught about cruelty and slavery and imperial looting, rather than about the many, many ways in which England, and the English, have made the world a better, more equitable, more attractive place.

How often are students told that there are more Englishmen on any list of the world's greatest individuals than there are representatives of any other nation? Isaac Newton. Charles Dickens. William Shakespeare. Isambard Kingdom Brunel. John Milton. Walter Raleigh. Geoffrey Chaucer. Charles Darwin. The list goes on and on.

For century after century England led the world in almost every conceivable branch of exploration, science and literature. England gave the world the Industrial Revolution. And it was England that did the leading, not Britain or the UK.

But for some time now everything good has been described as British and everything bad has been dismissed as English. Today's Britain is tolerant of everyone except the English. Under a cabal of Scottish leaders, and an EU desperate to see the end to the world's most successful nation, the English have been encouraged to apologise for their past, to deny their present and to accept that England has no future.

The simple (forgotten) truth is that in science, politics, industry and sport England has given the world more than any other country in the world.

Would an independent English parliament, composed of independent-minded English-born men and women, allow their history to be forgotten so easily?

Of course not.

70

'It was England that invented the forms of liberty that free people now call freedom.'
THE FINANCIAL TIMES

71

The Church of England, which has failed England and the English almost as much as the nation's politicians have done, has announced that it is considering demoting St George (England's national saint) and replacing him with someone called St Albans.

The reason?

The church is concerned that St George might be offensive to Muslims.

There has also been talk of removing St George's cross from the Union Jack.

And the Archbishop of Canterbury (whom one might reasonably expect to be concerned with defending English religious and legal traditions) has suggested that England should 'constructively accommodate' certain aspects of sharia law.

If the Church of England spent a little more time worrying about the interests of Christians, and a little less time worrying about the putative concerns of Muslims, it might find itself with a few more followers.

72

There is no doubt at all that the English would be much better off if the United Kingdom left the European Union. Leaving the EU would save England £60 billion a year (that is what our membership costs). That's £1,000 a year for every man, woman and child in the country. In addition, the red tape produced by Brussels now costs at least another £60 billion a year.

But there's a big problem with the UK leaving the EU: the majority of Scots and the Welsh think that the EU is wonderful.

They think it's wonderful for two reasons.

First, because they have over the last few years received a good deal of money from Brussels. (The money was, of course, merely a tiny percentage of the membership fee paid to the EU by England.)

Second, with pitiably childlike naivety, the Scots and the Welsh are convinced that the EU is helping them fight the English, and will enable them to achieve their dream of acquiring independence.

Many Scottish and Welsh politicians still seem unaware of the fact that the new parliaments which have been set up in their countries are not a prologue to independence but are, rather, merely an essential part of the creating of a European superstate.

Party politicians are committed to the European Union. They will, therefore, never approve of an English Parliament or an independent England.

Only a parliament of independent MPs would vote for such a change.

73

The Labour Governments which started their ruinous reign in 1997 have an appalling record on civil liberties. All governments are cynical conspiracies but the most recent incumbents have taken cynicism and conspiracy to new depths. Critics are either dismissed as paranoid, anarchic, nihilistic and (greatest irony of all) fascist, or are marginalised, arrested, tortured and imprisoned according to taste. Torture and surveillance seem to be considered 'normal' and 'acceptable' by a political party which seems obsessed with grandeur and legacy.

74

Whenever the Government feels itself threatened by yet another scandal the police miraculously find a nice new terrorist plot with which to terrify us all. A few suitable suspects are rounded up and thrown into prison. A few weeks later they are quietly released.

The French would riot at the slightest infringement of their liberties. The English, as a race, say and do nothing. A frightening number of people now actually want a state-sponsored economy.

How many people would protest if Brown suggested branding numbers on our foreheads, or putting surveillance cameras into our homes (all in the cause of protecting us against terrorism, money-laundering or television licence fee avoidance)?

75

In the aftermath of the attack on America which took place on the 11th September 2001 (known as the '11/9 attack') the British Government (like the American Government) gave itself far-reaching powers over ordinary citizens. The powers were taken (and sold to the electorate) as essential to defend both nations against a cruel, unseen enemy.

The truth, of course, is that the new dangers to Britain would never have occurred if Britain hadn't joined America's illegal war against Iraq.

Even so, the new powers never had anything to do with terrorism. The so-called 'war on terrorism' was merely an excuse, by an increasingly fascist government, to introduce new laws oppressing the ordinary people and suppressing any dissent.

Freedom, and free speech, are uncomfortable concepts for fascist governments run by politicians who are beholden to political parties.

It's far easier to control a nation when individual rights and freedom are kept to a minimum and collectivist slavery regarded as acceptable.

Collectivist slavery gives power to the few who choose to take it.

76

The English don't have, and never had, a constitution. But we used to have the Magna Carta. It was all we needed.

Today we have nothing: no bill of rights, no constitution and no Magna Carta.

Millions of people (politicians, civil servants and hangers-on) enthusiastically use the machinery of the State to benefit themselves: taking to themselves more and more power (and, also, more and more money) while our freedom to act and speak as we wish is rapidly diminished.

Can any politician in England be truly proud of the nation they have helped create? Of course they can't. They are, to a man and woman, greedy, self-serving traitors. Modern governments exist to protect the party rather than to protect the interests of the electorate.

Almost everything the Government now does is fascist – designed to support and strengthen the rights and powers of the State and to damage and weaken the rights and powers of individuals. We don't notice or appreciate what is happening because we have been misled, our attention has been diverted (as by a clever magician), our perceptions have been managed, and journalists have failed to enlighten us.

77

If you're going to support a political party it has to be the 'right' political party. As I write this I hear of a policeman being sacked for being a member of a legal and officially accepted political party. There is much talk of making some political parties illegal.

78

The Archbishop of York, Dr John Sentamu, has claimed that Britain is becoming a police state worthy of comparison with Uganda under Idi Amin.

Even a former director general of MI5 (Dame Stella Rimington) has warned that Britain is being pushed towards a police state. She won widespread support for her comment, though government ministers predictably dismissed the comment as 'abject nonsense' and, inevitably, accused the former MI5 chief of playing into the hands of terrorists with 'misguided talk'.

'If you're not with us, you're against us.'

79

The people didn't want to go to war with Iraq. Iraq hadn't threatened us. We aren't used to having to think of ourselves as bullies.

It was always clear that going to war with Iraq would dramatically increase – not reduce – the danger to individual citizens. (Decent countries don't start wars unless they are necessary for the defence of the realm.)

I believe that we went to war with Iraq because it suited Blair's personal agenda. Blair had the power to take us to war because the party political system gave him that power.

If we had a parliament full of independent MPs, history would have been quite different.

We would not have invaded Iraq or Afghanistan.

A poll of 2,246 adults in 2009 showed that 77% believe that the world has become a more frightening place since Labour came to power in 1997.

80

Governments used to exist (and ought to exist) to protect the population and to provide a basic infrastructure.

Modern politicians have encouraged people to expect their Governments to look after their every need.

Party politicians know that their chances of retaining power (and making money) are dependent on their maintaining control over as many aspects of our lives as possible.

In order to win elections political parties vie with one another to offer voters the most attractive package.

No one dares speak of individual responsibility or self-reliance. These are old-fashioned virtues which are widely regarded as being politically incorrect and, somehow, rather 'nasty'.

Our political leaders want to create an environment in which their multiculturalism and political correctness will grow. They want to make people terrified of a free market and of a horrible world in which people can make decisions for themselves and take responsibility for their own lives.

We are encouraged to believe that any improvements which have taken place in our lives are a result of big government and more regulations. This, of course, is not true. It's a case of the post hoc, ergo propter hoc fallacy. (Because B happened after A then B was caused by A. It is the same argument made by europhiles. They claim that it is because we're members of the European Union that there has not been a Third World War.)

81

In a healthy society people work to earn a living. Buying goods and services spreads the money around. Individuals decide how much they want to save and how much they want to spend. They also decide how they want to spend their money.

In our modern, unhealthy society the Government controls most of the money and hands it out to people it likes. Vote for us and we'll see you all right. All the political parties now have to make similar promises to stand a chance of succeeding at the next election.

82

Everything is falling apart. Our basic infrastructure is overstretched and underfunded. It isn't that we don't spend enough. The problem is that public money is wasted on the wrong things.

In March 2009, a survey conducted by the National Endowment for Science, Technology and the Arts, showed that 55% of 500 managers from across the public services believed that they would no longer be able to deliver an acceptable level of service within five years. A third believed that they would no longer be able to deliver an acceptable level of service within three years. In many areas of the country, services are already severely substandard. Hundreds of thousands of children leave primary school without basic numeracy and literacy skills. Scores of hospitals are so filthy dirty and badly run that the unfortunate patients who enter them are more at risk than if they'd stayed at home (or out in the street) and taken their chances.

During Labour's first decade in office Brown took £1 billion billion pounds out of the economy more than he would have taken if he'd allowed public expenditure to grow in line with inflation.

After a dozen years of Brown, the country has a failing infrastructure and a debt that will take generations to pay back. The debt will only be paid back through massive tax increases for years to come.

83

When we think party politicians are behaving stupidly we tend to say things like 'They can't be THAT stupid!'

But they can be. And they are.

Never underestimate the stupidity and greed of a professional party politician.

84

Governments should not run businesses or micromanage the economy. Governments have proved they are quite incapable of providing decent services of any kind. And yet the Government insists on controlling services such as health and education and on finding ways to punish those who prefer to obtain private services.

The micro-management, fascist, statist style of government favoured by the Labour party has led to another dramatic change in the way people behave.

The Government's programme of welfare support, and its blind enthusiasm for means-testing, mean that increasing numbers of people are now content to lie back and let their nation look after them. They demand and expect free care.

85

If you save money, or invest in a pension, then you will be punished when you are older by the Government's means-testing system. Means-testing helps redistribute wealth. This is good for the State because it gives the State more power, but bad for individuals because it eradicates freedom and ambition. Instead of encouraging and rewarding self-sufficiency the Government is encouraging dependence. This is not going to be easy to cure and is almost certain to get considerably worse before it gets better.

There are millions of citizens today who genuinely believe that the State owes them a living. They seem to assume that the State has a duty to provide them with money and services and they never seem to question the origin of either. Their dependence on the State is the reason for their loyalty to the State – and the controlling political party.

The State has taken responsibility for everything – education, health care, nursing – and has removed the survival instinct with which we should all protect ourselves.

Paradoxically, Big Government increases our liabilities (financial, legal and emotional) and exposes all our vulnerabilities.

The very basis of freedom is taking responsibility for your own life, but in England today millions seem prepared, even eager, to hand over all responsibility for themselves to the State. That's a waste of a life. Actually, it isn't living at all.

86

Local politics was always about favours. Now national politics is the same. Men and women don't join a political party to do things for the community; they join a political party to do things for themselves. Scroungers and cheats follow their example and also help themselves to money from the State's coffers. It is far easier than earning an honest living, and the State's coffers are seemingly never emptiable. Moreover, Politicians who were elected to look after the voters now expose the people they are paid to look after to increased danger (by starting wars).

Man's basic rights have been forgotten, buried under mounds of red tape and administration. The rights of the individual have been forgotten as the power of the party and the rights of the State have been expanded. Respect is but a memory.

It doesn't really matter whether you call it communism, statism, socialism or fascism: the names vary but the end result is absolutely the same.

87

What can one say about a Government which deliberately makes life more difficult for the potentially successful, while deliberately making life easier for the proven failures?

England has been destroyed by a potent and toxic mixture of statism, multiculturalism, political correctness, political self-interest, positive discrimination and an electoral system which has been hijacked by the political party system. The Government (and our local councils) have become too intrusive and too expensive in order to defend the interests of the party system.

Today, our governments ignore the things they should do while they interfere with the things they should leave alone. ('We can't stand by and do nothing,' is a constant cry from interfering politicians who would serve the people and the country better if they *did* stand by and do nothing.)

Politicians soothe us with slick but hollow promises and grand plans for the future but they are neither interested in, nor competent to deal with, the only thing we really want from them: solutions to the practical problems of nation management.

88

In their attempts to extend their control, party politicians take decisions in many areas where their interference really isn't needed. So, for example, they make decisions on moral issues, such as euthanasia and abortion, where they have no knowledge, experience or electoral jurisdiction.

It is almost obscene that a bunch of lying, cheating, amoral war criminals should dare even to consider talking publicly about moral issues – let alone passing laws designed to control our behaviour or our attitudes.

In the end they inevitably favour the views of whichever group shouts loudest, pushes hardest or has the deepest pockets. Ethical issues are decided for the nation in an intrinsically corrupt way. It is the role and responsibility of families and communities to improve moral standards. The idea that politicians (most of whom are scheming, thieving hypocrites) should dare offer guidance on moral matters is both contemptible and laughable.

89

Politicians now also interfere in our relationships and our every day activities.

Work, for example, is a partnership between employees and

employers. But in recent years the EU and the Labour Government (staffed largely by people who have never done a day of real work in their lives) have, inspired by their fascist dogma, made huge efforts to reduce the responsibilities of employees to virtually nothing and, at the same time, to enhance their rights. The results have been disastrous. No one – especially not employees – has benefited.

Politicians and civil servants are neither wise nor morally responsible. Their authority and reach have been allowed to grow unfettered when we would all be much better off if they were restricted.

90

When, in spring 2009, the Tories were in disarray over their promise to raise the inheritance tax threshold a spokesman said: 'This is a promise we intend to keep', thereby formally dividing political promises into those which are intended to be kept and those which are offered simply for display.

91

The Government terrifies us with an endless diet of manufactured fear. Politicians warn us that terrorists want to kill us. Politicians have belatedly (and suspiciously) embraced the threat of global warming and now they warn us that this threatens our very existence. And, as we shiver in fear, they soothe us by making a constant series of aspirational (and entirely meaningless) statements. We are going to cut carbon emissions by such and such a percentage by 2060. (The figure, which changes constantly, doesn't matter. No one takes it seriously.) All Britons will have access to an NHS dentist within three years. Fears and promises. Stick and carrot. Fears and promises. The end to boom and bust. Wars everywhere. A house for every family. Universal peace. New laws to protect us from money launderers. Bogeymen hiding behind the curtains. The electors are now harassed and blackjacked under a preposterous system of unintelligible laws which are contradictory and which exist only to give authority to small-minded men and women.

The Government is forever declaring things illegal and

attempting to stop people doing them. There is no discussion, no debate, no consideration of the options and the alternatives. The Government assumes that we are all witless children in need of an extensive framework of rules. What started out as a framework of laws, designed to protect us, quickly became a prison – confining and restricting.

92

The Government exists to administer (it is not by chance that the American Government is known as an Administration) but our politicians are incapable of administering. They are skilled at finding new ways to take money from us. And they are skilled, oh so very skilled, at finding ways to spend it in ways that will benefit them. But they have no interest in public service.

We have acquired, through their greed and our apathy, a Government which exists for its own benefit, rather than ours.

93

In the bad old days most of us had access to a GP and a bank manager we could trust and rely on. Our schools were full of teachers who understood the meaning of the word 'vocation'. Our streets were patrolled by policemen who cared about the communities they protected. We could go out without locking our doors. We had neighbours we could trust. We had neighbours who spoke the same language.

Today, we have an increasingly rigid society with increasing inequalities and a seemingly never-ending supply of rules and regulations.

The Government is introducing legislation requiring anyone travelling abroad to provide an exact itinerary in advance. Passport holding citizens will have to apply in advance for permission to go abroad. (And, presumably, if the trip is considered inappropriate or unnecessary then permission may be refused.) And Ministers are planning to use their computerised passport checking system to enable them to prevent people travelling if they have unpaid parking and speeding fines. Naturally, foreigners who wish to travel in or out of England will be able to do so without hindrance.

(It seems that Ministers have failed to read their passports recently. Inside each passport the wording still reads: 'Her Britannic Majesty's Secretary of State requests and requires…all those whom it may concern to allow the bearer to pass freely without let or hindrance'.)

94

I have no doubt that the credit crunch will be used as an excuse (opportunity might be a more appropriate word) to introduce a mass of new regulations and legislation.

Every threatening incident is used as an excuse to turn the screw and oppress us still further. And just as the American incident of 11/9 is now generally accepted to have been a home-grown incident designed to facilitate the introduction of oppressive new legislation in America, so it seems increasingly possible (bizarre as it sounds) that the whole credit crunch crisis just might have been allowed to happen in order to give the politicians an excuse to introduce more regulations controlling our financial affairs.

The financial problems which have destroyed so many pensions were caused by greedy bankers, incompetent regulators and reckless, stupid politicians who spent, spent spent and encouraged the electors to borrow, borrow, borrow in order to create a convincing mirage of wealth. And yet I guarantee that the regulations, the incoming legislation, will punish savers and workers rather than the bankers, the regulators or the politicians.

95

The fundamental ideal standing behind Plato's Republic and More's Utopia was equality. Both men believed that all citizens should have equal opportunities, and that a society should be governed solely with regard for the moral and material welfare of its citizens. How far we now are from that principle.

Through their allegiance to a toxic mixture of means-testing, political-correctness and multiculturalism our politicians have created a deeply unjust society.

Today it is the scroungers, the feckless, the lazy, the greedy and the crooked who are the chosen ones, and the hard working and the decent who are down-trodden and oppressed.

96

A citizen who wrote to Jacqui Smith when she was the Home Secretary, criticising her for creating a police state, was called for an interview with his GP. The GP had received a letter from the Fixated Threat Assessment Centre (FTAC) following instructions from the Home Office. The GP was required to interview the citizen who had dared to complain, in order to establish his 'state of mind'.

It seems that in future anyone who dares to criticise the Government in general, or the Home Secretary in particular, may be regarded as mentally ill.

The FTAC is a joint initiative by the Home Office, the Metropolitan Police and the Department of Health and consists of nine police officers (one chief inspector, one inspector, one sergeant and six police constables), three psychiatric nurses, a part time psychiatrist and a part time pathologist. The NHS component of this merry little quango costs over £500,000 a year.

The purpose of the FTAC is: 'to assess and manage the risks posed by those who engage in inappropriate or threatening forms of contact towards people in public life and in doing so, to direct severely mentally ill people, who are identified through such contacts, to the care that they so desperately need.'

FTAC may make use of police powers under section 136 of the Mental Health Act 1983 to 'take a person who appears to be suffering from a mental disorder, and in immediate need of care or control, to a place of safety'.

Officially, FTAC is described as 'a new form of diversion initiative in which the interests of patient care overlap with those of crime prevention'.

If you haven't gone cold inside by the time you have read this far then you may not be aware of the way that the Soviet Union and the East Germans used mental hospitals and psychiatric clinics to silence protestors and dissidents.

Naturally, the FTAC does not define what is considered 'inappropriate' or 'threatening' forms of contact. It is inappropriate or threatening because 'they' say it is.

The technique of branding outspoken individuals as 'mad' isn't new. But it's truly terrifying to see it being used in England, with the idea of troublesome individuals being sectioned as mentally ill and locked up where they can be controlled and silenced.

The FTAC has been given sweeping powers to check the files of thousands of suspects. And the team has the power to order that suspects undergo involuntary 'treatment' in secure psychiatric units. Troublesome citizens can be locked up for an indefinite period without trial, without criminal charges being laid and without any evidence of any crime being committed.

Our protectors have become our brutalisers and our leaders have led us into a barren wilderness where only the weeds of deceit and corruption flourish.

97

Hope and respect and loyalty have been replaced with fear, regrets, disappointments and missed opportunities. We have acquired an unmanageable burden of cares, responsibilities, commitments, resentments and debts: a smorgasbord of deliberately constructed nightmares. If we protest or complain or question then our protests, complaints and questions are dismissed as racist or sexist or otherwise unacceptable. The protestor is dismissed as an ungrateful troublemaker.

Anyone who dares to stand up and ask a question is a criminal; to be watched very carefully.

98

There are terrorists everywhere. We must watch out for them. They seem normal, you see, but they ask questions. The Government has encouraged snitches and tittle tattle and gossip. If you want to say something nasty about someone, get them into endless trouble, all you have to do is ring one of the Government's many free helplines.

'You don't have to be sure,' says one Government advertisement. 'If you suspect it, report it.'

They promise us a better future but in truth they are only concerned about a better future for them, not us.

(As an aside it is worth mentioning that the Government spends £400 million of our money each year on advertising. Much of the advertising is designed to promote the interests of the ruling party.)

99

When the economy does well, and house prices rise on a sea of debt, national politicians take the credit. Beaming smiles, modest nods, much talk of the rewards of prudence. When the economy does badly the same politicians blame global problems over which they have no control. No one exemplifies this better than Gordon Brown.

Brown constantly promised to save us from economic disasters which had been created by hedge funds, short-sellers, offshore tax havens and the inventors of the subprime mortgage.

Our financial crisis was nothing to do with him or his policies, of course. How could we think such a thing. He may have been in charge of the economy but he took no responsibility for the problems we faced. Shame on us for even thinking that it might be so.

100

Scotsman Brown, party politician, gave billions of pounds of English taxpayers' money to save two Scottish banks which should have been allowed to go bust. Would he have spent so much to save two English banks? It's enough to make any English-born patriot scream with frustration and pain.

101

The Scottish Claim of Rights states: 'We...do hereby declare and pledge that in all our actions and deliberations (the) interests (of the Scottish people) shall be paramount.'

The Scottish Claim of Rights has been signed and approved by (among others) Gordon Brown, Alistair Darling and the former speaker, Michael Martin.

102

Confession. I don't like modern party politicians. They are offensive, crooked, egocentric, narcissistic and hypocritical. They are composed of gristle and tripe. They have no hearts or brains let alone souls or spirits. And I despise people who work for the Government because they are the people who would operate the gas chambers partly for the fun of it and partly for a guaranteed index-linked non-contributory pension. Just thought I'd mention it. So that you know where I stand. I don't want there to be any doubt.

103

Theoretically, the Government and its agents are there to protect our freedom and to enable us to go about our daily business safely and without restraint. That's it. But that is now exactly the opposite to what they do. Time and time again they act out of personal interest and greed. Taxes are rising inexorably and the quality of public services is in a deep decline. During Brown's tenure in Government our taxes rose two and a half times faster than our earnings. This was done so that Labour could buy votes with a spending spree designed to hire voters for the party (as employees or as dependants). The Government merrily ignored the evidence which showed clearly that once the State sector spends more than 40% of a nation's income then the nation's economic performance deteriorates dramatically.

104

If you work for an hour then for between fifteen and twenty four minutes of the hour you are working for the Government. (With National Insurance payments it's probably nearer twenty to thirty minutes of every hour).

What do we get for this?

We get armies which fight wars we don't want fighting and which expose us to great danger. We get a National Health Service which is so poorly run that it kills more people than it saves. We get schools that are so poorly managed that huge numbers of young people leave school unable to read or write, while parents who can scrape together the wherewithal pay to send their children to private schools. We get roads but we must pay more if we want to use them. We get a public transport network which is the most inefficient and expensive in the world. We get politicians and civil servants who pay themselves extraordinarily well, and do very little work. We get expensive membership of the European Union – a membership that brings us absolutely nothing but trouble and costs. We get a corrupt and incompetent police force which is concerned more with making money, filling in forms and obeying the strictures of the politically correct than in protecting people or property. We pay for a vast army of busy bodies who never tire of telling us what we can and cannot do.

105

It is our individual responsibility, as defined by law, by history and by common sense, to ensure that we pay as little tax as possible. That is our responsibility to our families and ourselves. The Government doesn't see it that way. As far as they are concerned what is ours is theirs and what is theirs is also theirs. Nice.

What the politicians don't realise (never having worked for a living) is that if taxes go up too much people will put most of their creative effort into avoiding taxes, rather than doing what they do. An increasing number of people are now so fed up with taxes that they are working part time – cutting living expenses and cutting tax bills.

106

If you win money on the lottery there is no tax to pay. If you work hard and save hard you pay tax on your earnings and your savings. The unmistakeable message is that the Government disapproves of work and saving, and encourages gambling.

107

The principle of taxing heavily and giving money back to people in allowances is favoured because it gives the State more control over our lives.

108

Everything we do needs a licence. And every time we need a licence we must pay the Government more money. Today you even need a licence if you want to sing Happy Birthday to a friend in your local pub.

109

The State is selling our roads to private companies so that the companies can rent them back to us when we want to use them. They're our roads. We paid for them to be built. Now someone else owns them and we pay to use them.

Did anyone ask you if this would be OK?

They didn't ask me, either.

110

Politicians everywhere are corrupt and self-serving. And England, a once proud nation with a vast history, is about to disappear.

Most English people don't know what is happening to their country. England is full of sleeping princes and princesses. Anyone who relies upon the Biased Broadcasting Corporation (the BBC) or the national press for information will be well educated about the McCanns, the size of Jordan's breasts and the decline of the English football team. But they may not understand that successive governments have deliberately signed treaties which allow England to be torn apart and recreated as anonymous administrative regions.

Modern governments deliberately hide the truth from us as much as they possibly can. And, because we have a poor media, we rarely find out things we are really entitled to know.

The mainstream media generally only report demonstrations,

events and revelations which fit their agenda (or, more often, the Government's agenda). Any suggestion that we enjoy a free press and live in a free country is laughable.

111

The real task of journalists is constantly to embarrass and frequently to terrify the comfortable, complacent members of the establishment. This happens too rarely. I have, over the years, worked for most national newspapers and broadcast media in the UK and the one thing that has always worried me is the way that journalists invariably become part of the establishment; too often supporting, protecting and defending the party political system.

News is the stuff that people don't want printed.

112

The Labour Party promised to be free and open. It has been neither. It produced a Freedom of Information Act but the result has been that obtaining vital information is now even more difficult than it was under the last Conservative Government.

113

Everything civil servants and politicians do should be out in the open. We pay salaries (and fat pensions) to our civil servants and politicians. That makes them our employees. Why, therefore, should they have secrets from us? Aren't we entitled to know what they are doing in our name and with our money?

114

Philosophy, purpose and passion are sadly lacking from today's miserable posse of MPs. Look around Parliament and you will see rows of incompetent hypocrites, smug deceivers and malignant conspirators. These people may be stupid, but they are not harmless. They pose a very real, continuing and ever increasing threat to our freedom.

115

Speaking in America, Gordon Brown, in full sanctimonious mood, boasted that his father was a Minister of the Church and called on the Americans to 'celebrate men and women of integrity who treat people fairly'. As he spoke, his own back room boys were cooking up a plot to spread obscenities about Tory ministers. And his ministers and MPs were furnishing and decorating their homes with taxpayers' money. The Scot who boasts about prudence and saving the world has turned England into a banana republic.

We are entitled to politicians who inspire us, who respect the truth and who exhibit dignity and integrity. But, under the party system, these qualities simply aren't available. These are unavailable luxuries: caviare and vintage champagne. Instead, we must make do with stale bread and dirty water.

There is no room for integrity in public life today. It's been squeezed out by avarice. The party system has destroyed political honesty and it has destroyed impartiality and the concept of public service among civil servants.

In the face of widespread corruption we are powerless and disenfranchised.

116

'A democracy cannot survive as a permanent form of government. It can last only until its citizens discover that they can vote themselves largesse from the public treasury. From that moment on, the majority (who vote) will vote for those candidates promising the greatest benefits from the public purse, with the result that a democracy will always collapse from loose fiscal policies, always followed by a dictatorship.'
LORD THOMAS MACAULEY (1800–1859)

117

True liberty means having the right to have our own thoughts and to share them with others, freely and openly. Liberty means having the right to spend our days in the way that we want to spend them, as long as what we do does not impinge on the rights of others.

Liberty means that a man should be able to run his life, and his business, in the way that he thinks it should be run, as long as it does not interfere with the rights of others to do the same thing. Liberty means that communities can choose their own leaders and decide how they want their children to be educated, their hospitals to be organised and so on.

Today, liberty is something we read about in history books.

Together the professional party politicians have created an angry, mean, resentful, rude, ungrateful, violent world.

A plague on all their parties!

The party politicians have terrified us into submission.

According to a recent report called *Perspectives on a changing society* an overwhelming majority of the public are willing to give up freedom to combat the threat of terrorism. Eight in ten citizens think that it is acceptable for the police to tap telephones and to open the mail. It is, they believe, 'a price worth paying'. Though I'm not sure they know just what they think they are getting for the price they are paying.

A quarter of the population think that torturing terror suspects is justified. Nearly half think it's fine to deny suspects the right to a jury trial.

Eight out of ten citizens now think that compulsory identity cards are a price worth paying. (The word compulsory has become one of the most commonly used in our language. Am I the only person who always finds it irritating?) A third think it is acceptable to ban peaceful protests and demonstrations. Henry David Thoreau once wrote that the mass of men lead lives of quiet desperation. Nothing but desperation could lead men and women to believe that freedom is a disposable asset. The Government wants to bully, exhaust and frighten us so that we don't believe that there is any hope that we can change things.

'What's the use, nothing is going to change?' is for most people, the only way to survive. After all, we are all suspects now.

118

I've fought for years for things I believe in. It has been exhausting and, I admit with sadness, largely pointless.

Today, fighting injustice has become harder than ever. The red tape has become virtually impenetrable. Most people don't care or have any fight left (or they have been brainwashed into believing that the system is right, that the politicians are doing their best and the bureaucrats are just doing their jobs).

But, I do believe that we can succeed through the bloodless revolution described in this book.

119

All forms of hierarchical authority are intrinsically corrupt. Those with authority need to be given as little power as possible, and need to be watched constantly by those on whose behalf their authority is exercised.

120

It was the clerks and bureaucrats who gave Hitler his power. It is the clerks and bureaucrats who give the EU fascists their power. And it is the clerks and bureaucrats who give England's fascists their power.

121

Instead of protecting us our Government has become our greatest enemy; establishing slavery instead of protecting our freedom; endangering us instead of safeguarding us; and creating uncertainty (through reams of legislation, some of it retrospective and much of it so vague that it can be interpreted at will by bureaucrats).

Free speech is stifled and peaceful demonstrators who dare to tell the truth are arrested. Even heckling at political meetings has been outlawed.

Every public meeting should have someone at the back shouting out 'balls' to everything the speakers say. But these days you'd get arrested if you did. Complaints and protests are ignored.

Our totalitarian leaders are systematically destroying our liberties.

Today's politicians don't stand for anything but themselves. Scratch a politician and you'll find a large expense account and a yearning for self-aggrandisement. The mechanics of our electoral system means that we have all been disenfranchised by scores of political pygmies on the rampage down from Scotland.

122

The Government has created two societies: those who work for, and are paid by, the Government and the rest – those who only give money to the Government.

It is a two-tier society; two worlds, the givers and the takers.

Things reached the pinnacle of absurdity when the staff of the Financial Services Authority, the FSA, (the regulatory body which failed to do anything to stop the financial meltdown) gave themselves huge bonuses for failing so successfully, and a Home Secretary, Jacqui Smith, accidentally claimed the cost of two pornographic movies on her Parliamentary expenses.

Politicians seem more interested in gouging as much money as they can out of the public purse than they are in protecting what is left of our democracy. 'Don't forget to claim for the bath plug when you're filling in the expenses form, dear!'

123

The only crimes now regarded as truly serious are crimes against the Government or its officers; crimes which threaten the establishment (or its officers) in any way.

Burglars are allowed to stay out of prison. Muggers and murderers receive only the lightest of sentences; sometimes let off with a few, mild words of criticism, a token for some free CDs and a holiday.

But elderly citizens who refuse to pay their council tax (on the not unreasonable grounds that if they pay it they won't be able to afford to eat) are sent straight to prison. On the face of it this seems mad. And in a logical, caring, democratic world it would be. The burglar is clearly a much greater threat than the pensioner. But we live in a fascist world and in a fascist world it is the State, not the individual, whose interests must be protected.

This is practical fascism: the deadly marriage of capitalism and statism in which the fascists always come first. The burglar is no threat to the State but the person who doesn't pay tax is.

Hit an old man with a brick and you may walk free. Attack a policeman, now regarded as a servant of the State not the public, and you will go to prison for a long, long time.

You think I'm exaggerating? I'm not. A man who left a 96-year-old war veteran blind in one eye, after attacking him on a packed train, was given a three year supervision order. The man, who launched an unprovoked attack on the 96-year-old in Croydon, South London, was found guilty of grievous bodily harm after the attack was caught on closed circuit television.

124

Citizens who have retired are considered a nuisance and a drain on the State's resources. They contribute nothing and are, as far as the State is concerned, a waste of time and money. They are routinely denied the protection of the courts. Elderly patients in nursing homes can legally be drugged without their knowledge or approval. And the over 60's are denied medical attention because they are of little value to the State.

125

Governments controlled by party politicians have created a world in which those who run the country (and who work for the electorate) can do whatever they please while citizens can now only do what they are permitted to do. And that, of course, is the reverse of traditional English law, and the precise opposite of the type of freedom guaranteed by the Magna Carta and a whole host of subsequent legislation.

We have adopted EU law which says that private citizens can do what the bureaucrats say they can do and no more.

126

It is not the place of the Government to tell us that we must stop smoking or eat less. But these are responsibilities which the Government (inspired by the EU) has taken unto itself.

It is not the place of the Government to run banks or control water companies or trains or anything else that requires maintenance or a timetable.

The State should not run businesses. It is very bad at it. It should, at most, enact legislation designed to regulate (mildly) those businesses which are essential and laws to punish (severely) managers who are dishonest or seriously incompetent.

Nor, incidentally, should the State become involved in broadcasting or publishing. I believe that the BBC has done more damage to our democracy and our freedom than any other broadcasting institution. There is not a single journalist working for the BBC whom I would trust to edit a parish magazine. To a BBC journalist a scoop is something you use for ice cream. Because it has a vast, guaranteed income, a special tax which is not dependent on market forces, the BBC can pay huge amounts of money to celebrities and for the coverage of sports it wants to dominate. It can afford to throw money around quite recklessly. (In May 2009 the BBC responded to suggestions that, in view of the nation's economic state, the annual tax on viewing should not be raised, with all the shock and horror of a maiden aunt being propositioned. The very notion that they should cut the nearly £25 million they spend on hotels sent BBC managers into a swoon. Unemployment figures may soar but BBC staff must have their bonuses, their taxis and their unthreatened lifestyle.) Commercial broadcasters, unable to match the BBC's spending power, must resort to making ever more desperate programmes in an attempt to grab ratings: the result is an inevitable lowering of broadcasting standards. The BBC spends £145 million a year of licence-fee payers' money on its website where material is available free to anyone who wants to use it (whether they are licence fee payers or not). The result is that commercial websites cannot charge for material and so cannot survive.

Similarly, local councils which publish newspapers do enormous damage to the freedom of speech and the democratic process by putting private publications out of business.

127

Meritocracy once drove progress and social justice by allowing poor youngsters to rise through grammar schools and challenge the traditional upper class. But this was considered to be a bad thing and so comprehensive schools were founded so that the school system could be dumbed down to the lowest common denominator.

So that all children could be the same and no one would fail, exams were made easier.

Teachers were told not to correct mistakes made in the classroom lest this make some children feel less adequate.

School sports were abandoned for the same reason (giving local councils an opportunity to make a good profit by selling off the playing fields as building land).

128

Small day to day decisions are taken from us by bureaucrats applying endless rafts of legislation which no one ever understands. It is no wonder that when it comes to the big decisions we are happy to leave those to others too. We are like unfortunate children; oppressed by fear and violence.

Governments should provide comfort, support and reassurance; instead they concentrate on frightening people half to death in order to keep them cowed and in their place.

The politicians have stolen our freedom and our rights against our wishes, without ever bothering to ask our approval. For over a decade, the Labour Party (a good chunk of them a raiding party from north of the border) did the stealing. Leading members of the other two parties stood idly by, wondering how they could get invited to the party too. No one stuck up for us, the people.

129

The truth is that today, the Government is the biggest source of terrorism in our lives; the terrorism of state control, the erosion of all our traditional values and the replacement with oppressive laws allegedly designed to protect us from violence but in practice designed to introduce a reign of terror similar to that which followed the French Revolution.

The annual cost of new Government and EU regulations is £77 billion. The *annual* cost. We are so overladen with laws that the law itself has become meaningless. Publicly expressed opinions can now be against the law. Thinking of what is or might be illegal can itself be illegal. People are arrested and put in prison for their contemplations.

130

The Government proudly advertises the fact that it now crushes cars owned by citizens who don't pay their road tax. This is, of course, quite mad. It is a terrible waste of energy and an insult to the environment. But the State crushes cars because it can and because it serves to frighten other citizens and to remind them that not paying taxes has terrifying consequences.

131

The political parties have given us a world in which a passer-by dare not push a child on a swing, in which a householder dare not admonish yobs who are throwing rubbish onto his garden or urinating in his doorway, in which travellers are treated like criminals and where making a joke can put you into prison.

They have given us a world in which criminals who are let out of our overcrowded prisons early are given cash to compensate them for the loss of free food and lodging. So far the Labour Government has freed 50,000 criminals and paid them £5 million in compensation. I kid you not.

They have given us a world in which most new jobs created since 1997 have been filled by workers born outside Europe. They have given us a world in which a woman can earn more by having a child and signing on for benefits than she could earn as a cook or a hairdresser or a waitress.

They have given us a world in which many people on welfare receive more money than hard-working citizens on minimum wages.

They have given us a world in which England has more people on welfare than Ireland has citizens, and a world in which the Welfare State specialises in keeping people on benefits for ever.

They have given us a world in which every time we commit a crime we give them a chance to take, and store, our DNA. And since they have criminalised almost everything ('everything which is not specifically allowed is against the law') they have many opportunities to criminalise us.

132

I gave a pound coin to a beggar the other day. As I walked on I heard a shout. I turned round and saw him sneering and waving two fingers. Society is like that now. We give. But it's never enough.

133

Have you ever wondered why so many beggars on the streets have dogs?

There are two reasons (if we put aside the thought that maybe they just love animals).

The first is that having a dog attracts sympathy and money from passers-by. But the second, and possibly most significant, is that individuals claiming benefits receive around £10 a week extra for each dog they own (or claim they own).

Do hard-working citizens receive money from the State to enable them to buy dog food?

Apparently not.

134

They tell us that to safeguard our freedom we must sacrifice it. We cannot enjoy it unless we give it away. We have become slaves.

You think that my use of the word 'slave' sounds a little over-stated?

Think about it for a moment.

We work for them. We do what we are told. We have no control over our lives.

My dictionary definition of a slave is 'a person who is forced to obey another; a person who is controlled'.

135

To describe the UK today as a democracy is as absurd as it would be to describe it as a free country. We have lost our freedom. The people who run the country no longer do what we want.

Did you want them to give untold billions to save the bonuses of the rich and stupid bankers? Do you know anyone who did?

Did you want Brown to sign the Lisbon Treaty without the referendum he had promised? Do you know anyone who did?

Did you want our country to start wars against two countries which had never threatened us? Do you know anyone who did?

They run the country for them not us. They ignore what we want. And they treat us like slaves.

136

Politicians since 1997 have corrupted endlessly and destroyed morality in public life. It is not the bankers or the regulators or the civil servants who have ruined Britain (though they have all played their parts with great enthusiasm) but the politicians. And anything other than a complete overhaul of our political system will prove inadequate and disappointing.

137

Here's a curious fact: of the seven men who gave more than £1,000,000 to the Labour Party during Blair's decade in power, six ended up in the House of Lords. Now, there's a coincidence for you.

138

It is hardly surprising that millions of educated and intelligent people now waste their lives watching terrible television programmes as a nightly relief from the daily struggles with bureaucracy and corporate inefficiency.

Television is the opiate of the people.

'Economic freedom is based on a simple moral rule: everyone has a right to his or her life and property, and no one has the right to deprive anyone of these things,' wrote Ron Paul, former USA Presidential candidate.

If you burst into a neighbour's home and demanded money you would be regarded as a bad person. Even if you insisted that you were going to use the money to help feed starving children you would still be thought of as a bad person. Robin Hood is really only acceptable when he's dressed in green tights and camping in the woods.

There's only one time when theft is legal. And that's when governments do it.

Because they back up their demands with threats ('If you don't give us your money we will kidnap you and lock you up') and physical intimidation (men in uniforms, carrying weapons, can be pretty intimidating) we allow our Government to demand money from us without ever thinking deeply about the legality or morality of what they are doing.

Statists believe the State has the right to initiate force against its own citizens to make them do what it wants them to do.

When our Government demands money from us it has a lot of back up: tax inspectors, policemen, courts and bailiffs. Behind them stand the army, the navy, the airforce and nuclear weapons. In other words: force.

Taxes are, at their simplest, protection money. We pay taxes not necessarily because we believe they are worthwhile, or because we believe that the money will be spent on improving society, but because we know that we will be punished if we don't pay up.

Everything the Government does depends on thuggery. It's a bit like the mob. The mob threatens to harm you or take your property if you don't give them protection money. The Government threatens to harm you or take your property if you don't pay your taxes.

The basic principle of income tax is that the Government owns us; we work for it and it is entitled to take what it wants from what we earn. The fact that we are allowed to keep a percentage of our earnings is a favour more than a right. Income tax is the basic weapon of the statist. Those who pay income tax are being used as forced labour for several months of every year. Income tax may well be an obligation but it is not a responsibility.

If I were to send you letters demanding that you give me a big chunk of your earnings you would consider me a dangerous criminal. If I persisted with my demands, and started threatening that if you didn't give me a big chunk of your money I would come into your home and take what I wanted and then also take you from your home and lock you in a small room, you would consider me even more dangerous and even more of a criminal. You would probably think I was mad.

But that's precisely what the civil servants working for the Government do all the time. In their eyes we are all criminals; guilty of tax fraud until proven innocent. They demand money with menaces. If they did it as private citizens they would be locked up. But because they do it on behalf of the State what they do is perfectly legal.

In a dozen long years the witless Scot, Gordon Brown, has turned one of the world's fairest and simplest tax systems into one of the least fair and certainly into the most complicated. (And complicated tax systems create more problems, produce more unfairness, result in more loopholes and waste more productive time on filling in forms than simple tax systems.)

Her Majesty's Revenue and Customs (HMRC) can demand information, raise assessments, enter premises and enforce payment on grounds that would not be allowed in any criminal prosecution. Moreover, since HMRC are pretty lax when it comes to dealing with confidential data, information given to HMRC can no longer be regarded as private.

Those who take (the politicians and the scroungers) forget that the State produces nothing and that every penny that is distributed must first be taken from a man or woman who has worked, produced and saved.

The hard-working citizen has become the forgotten man, doomed for ever to pay for the excesses of governments and scroungers.

140

'The Government is set to borrow more in the next two years than the total borrowing Labour inherited in 1997, dating back to 1691.'
FINANCIAL TIMES MARCH 26TH 2009

141

The Government is making legislation retrospective. The result must surely be that people will be sent to prison for things that weren't illegal when they did them.

142

According to one whistle-blower, post to the Inland Revenue often just 'gets binned'. Why am I not surprised, let alone shocked? Complaints to the Independent Adjudicator's Office have doubled since 2005. When Her Majesty's Revenue and Customs (HMRC) wants money it thinks it is owed (and tax collectors smell a bonus in the air) then the letters come thick and fast (with deadlines attached). But when HMRC has made a mistake, owes money or is being asked for a clarification it often appears that no one is interested. After my father's death the solicitor handling the closure of what should have been a simple and straightforward estate told me that there was a delay because the tax office had told her that they had a backlog of three months worth of mail. In practice this meant that it was taking them three months to open and read a letter. (They managed to speed things up considerably when I threatened to make a formal complaint.)

143

Just about everything you or I do these days is taxed. In order to convince the more simple-minded electors that he wasn't putting up taxes Brown introduced a vast armoury of stealth taxes. We need to pay the Government special taxes if we want to get married, drive a car, own a car, travel abroad, buy a house, invest our savings, leave our savings uninvested in the bank, watch television or die. And, of course, every charge that a Government introduces is steadily increased, year after year. Governments start with a small fee and say that it is just going to be a nominal charge, but that's just a lie, of course. For example, when prescription charges were introduced in 1968 they were 2/6 (12.5p). In April 07 they went up to £6.85. That's a rise of over 5,000%. If prescription charges had followed the retail price index they would now be at £1.45. (Only the English pay prescription charges. The Welsh and the Scots receive their medicines free of charge – paid for, of course, by English taxpayers.)

144

In the private sector, failure usually leads to a diminution in power and wealth. With the exception of banks and bankers, companies or individuals who are bad at their jobs, and fail to satisfy public demands and needs, get paid less. Profits and authority fall.

In the public sector the exact opposite happens. Public institutions which are failing receive more money. They are rewarded for incompetence.

145

Very little of the money raised in taxes is used to improve the quality of life in England or to help people who are genuinely in need. Instead, much of it is given to civil servants, politicians and quango sitters as salaries, pensions, expenses and bonuses.

Taxpayers no longer control how their money is spent, and the way politicians spend tax money is now utterly divorced from the wishes of the taxpayers, who provide the money in the first place.

The Government has attracted a mass of camp followers and the nation's wealth is being wasted on supporting an ever-growing network of gravy trains, carrying hundreds of thousands of highly-paid and well-pensioned incompetents and unemployables. Party politicians have created a vast number of quangos which provide well-paid employment, and a considerable amount of power, for those who support, protect and defend the party. To add insult to injury these are invariably not only receiving huge salaries and fees and expenses but are also paid massive bonuses for failing to do what they were hired to do.

It is absurd that the bonus culture has permeated the civil service. In 2009 staff at the Treasury, all on large salaries and hugely satisfactory pensions, received bonuses worth £27 million. What on earth for? Their job is running the economy. The economy is in tatters.

Policemen get bonuses. So do Olympics organisers, Post Office employees and BBC managers. Greed, as originated in the banks, has now become government-approved.

It has become too easy for public sector workers to become rich without effort or risk.

In addition, much of our money is given to scroungers who choose not to work. And a great deal of it is given to the European Union as our annual membership fee. Huge amounts are spent on waging war against countries which have never threatened us. Very, very little of it is spent on feeding starving children.

146

Treasury officials and quango bosses spend billions without any reference to our elected representatives as though the money they are spending is somehow different to the money they themselves earn, spend and save.

State spending as a proportion of our nation's Gross Domestic Product (GDP) has now reached 49%. That means that the Government now controls half our economy – so much for the idea that we live in a capitalist or entrepreneurial society. In the northeast of England, State spending accounts for 66.4% of GDP. In Wales it is 71.6% and in Northern Ireland it is a staggering 77.6%. Not even the Soviet Republic managed to achieve that amount of State dominance.

Politicians and civil servants waste our money in all sorts of ways. They spent £750 million on the Dome. We pay £21 million a mile to build motorways. How can you spend that much on a piece of road?

The police are so inefficient that the cost of holding a prisoner in a police cell was, in March 2009, £853 a night. (To put this in perspective, a night in a superior suite at the Ritz hotel in London cost £805 including taxes).

It is perhaps not surprising, therefore, that the police put so much effort into raising money from taxpayers – rather than remaining content with 'serving and protecting'. In addition to the millions raised by speed cameras (proven to cause more accidents than they prevent and, therefore, clearly simply a money raising exercise) the police even use premium rate lines to enable them to charge the public money for telephone calls. Citizens who dial an 0845 number to report a non-emergency crime to the police are likely to end up paying for the privilege. Bizarrely, inexplicably and utterly indefensibly, police forces in England actually make money out of people reporting crime. This is utter madness.

In Edinburgh the new Scottish Regional Parliament building, built to house the European Union's regional parliament, was originally estimated to cost £10 to £14 million but it ended up costing English taxpayers a staggering £414 million.

An astonishing £400,000 was spent on designing a logo for the London Olympics. In March 2009 the Ministry of Defence spent £900,000 on 3,150 office chairs so that flat bottomed clerks could sit around in luxury while soldiers in Afghanistan were reduced to lending one another combat gear – or buying it themselves.

Billions (literally) are wasted on doomed computer schemes.

Everything the Government plans ends up costing ten, twenty, a hundred times as much as the official estimate. It is our money and so it doesn't count. Politicians spend other people's money as though it were, well, other people's money. And politicians (and journalists) dismiss potential savings of £50 million or £500 million as 'insignificant'.

In the strange world occupied by party politicians and civil servants, a pound of 'other people's money' isn't worth anywhere near as much as a pound of your own money. People who would spend a day looking for a lost fiver will happily sneer at £100 million of public money and dismiss it as 'small change'.

147

In our hearts we know that the Government is wasting our money and that the bureaucracy it has built up is doing far more harm than good, but how do we set about changing things?

The politicians and the bureaucrats control things and they aren't ever likely to change the system they have created. Why would they? Modern bureaucracies have a vested interest in maintaining themselves. Their effort is put into protecting themselves and their budget. They know that the best way to get a bigger budget and more power is to employ more people. And so it goes on.

That is exactly what is wrong with the National Health Service today; it exists not to care for patients but to provide secure employment for the employees.

148

Those who insist on meddling in our lives have proved time and time again that they aren't very good at it and that, in the long run, their priorities are selfish rather than altruistic. They spend a fortune hiring armies of Labour voters to teach people how to eat less, how to wash their hands, how to fold disposable nappies or how to eat five portions of fruit a day. They pay huge salaries for this sort of nonsense; £50,000 a year with an index-linked pension, expenses (and quite possibly a good bonus for turning up if the weather is inclement) is probably not exceptional in the hand-washing-training business.

149

During the global economic crisis of 2007 and 2008, while other countries were cutting back and trying to reduce their State payroll obligations, Brown was steadily increasing Britain's State payroll. It isn't difficult to see why: every new employee is another loyal voter. We pay the bills. The politicians reap the benefits.

150

Greedy bankers and incompetent regulators can be blamed in part for the financial crisis which hit Britain in 2007 and 2008 but the politicians must take the greater share of the blame. (Although they don't and won't, of course. We live in a blame society unless you work for the Government).

Party politicians have drained money from the economy to run massive, untested, unproductive programmes of social engineering and they have donated billions of pounds of our money to the European Union.

We have been destroyed by statism, multiculturalism, political correctness, our slavish following of American imperialism, the self-interest of our politicians and public servants, institutional racism (with the white citizens as the victims) and a corrupt and unrepresentative electoral system.

151

One basic principle politicians invariably ignore is that when the Government (or a council) spends our money it should do so for our benefit and not for their benefit. If a hospital is short of money then what money there is should be spent on patients and not on staff (and especially not on administrators). But too many hospitals build new office blocks and spend a fortune on furnishings when patients are dying for need of another X-ray machine. This happens because hospitals (like governments) are run for the benefit of the staff rather than the people paying the bills. It's what happens when you separate payment and service.

152

Another often ignored basic principle is that the Government and councils should always endeavour to look at the big picture when taking decisions.

When snow fell in England in early 2009, many councils said that they could not afford to put grit on the roads. This was short-sighted and stupid and exhibited nothing more than simple incompetence. Not gritting the roads leads to accidents. And, in addition to the personal consequences, this leads to health costs and business losses.

If they don't want to buy grit and keep it for snowy days (and the stuff is hardly likely to go past its sell-by-date is it?) councils should keep a contingency fund for emergencies so that they can buy grit to put on the roads when it is likely to be needed (during the winter, for example).

Instead of hiring vast numbers of unnecessary and unwanted new members of staff (to aid their empire building ambitions) council bosses should simply put some money aside to help them deal with emergency problems.

Similarly, it may cost more to do motorway repairs at night (because the workmen have to be paid extra and lights have to be provided) but the saving to the community is enormous when road delays are minimised.

None of this requires much more than basic common sense, and an understanding that central and local governments exist to serve the greater and smaller communities and not to pander to the personal whims of their employees.

153

We should rage at our oppression, our disappearing freedoms and the way we and our country are being abused. We should stand up and protest at the way we are treated without respect by the people whom we pay to serve us.

Lying politicians and government employees have created a problem which is not going to go away. People don't believe anything the Government says, whether it's about terrorism, expenses or childhood vaccinations. Trust has gone; it will not be easily restored.

The basic problem is that the people who go into politics, and the civil service, are intrinsically self-serving and corrupt. They enter public service not out of a sense of duty, or a desire to improve the world, but because they believe (not without good reason) that public service is the best way to achieve wealth and power.

In order to defend ourselves, we need to cut down on the power of Government and the amount of our money it has to spend.

We have to reassess the whole nature of politics, the purpose of government and the power we should vest in the people we elect to govern on our behalf.

Hell will freeze over before our current batch of politicians do the 'right' thing (even if they ever know what the 'right' thing is). And so we have to stand up for ourselves and take back the power which is rightly ours. We need a revolution.

A traditional revolution is, of course, impossible in a country where innocent visitors can be shot in the head without so much as a warning, where a woman can be arrested for reading out the names of British soldiers killed in the illegal invasion of Iraq and where frail octogenarians are forced to remove their shoes and surrender their nail clippers before being allowed to board their holiday flight.

There isn't much chance of battalions of aggrieved citizens being allowed onto the streets to overthrow the Government. Violence is not an option which is open to us (even if we wanted to take it).

A government which sends tanks to Heathrow airport to make a point, and which allows policemen to beat up innocent, peaceful protestors will not hesitate to use force to defend its position.

We need another type of revolution: a bloodless revolution.

154

The revolution won't involve the scrounging classes. The scrounging classes will only protest about the price of petrol or taxes (such as the poll tax) which are likely to affect them. (The poll tax, the most sensible piece of new tax legislation in generations, was thrown out because a small section of scroungers didn't like the idea of having to pay something towards the services they enjoy.) The scroungers won't protest about things which threaten our past, our culture, our freedom, our present and our future.

The scrounging classes won't rebel against the State because they receive their money from the State. They are quite comfortable, thank you very much, and unwilling to bite the hand that is feeding them so generously.

155

We need honest men and women to go to Parliament, on our

behalf, and to discuss issues relating to our lives. We need local, county and national representatives. We don't need leagues or treaties with foreign powers (Thomas More saw the danger of these – he excluded all treaties with foreign powers from his Utopia). We need a few simple laws and a system for ensuring they are obeyed.

156

We need sanitation services and fresh water supplies. We need wide, tree-lined streets. Every home should have a garden. Hospitals and schools should be organised and run locally. Children should be educated and given skills and crafts (men and women who do work which requires skill obtain much more satisfaction, pride and happiness from their lives).

We want to live in a Christian country celebrating Christian values, which include tolerance. We want a country where people speak one language (English).

157

The revolution will come, as revolutions always do, from the middle classes.

It is the honest, hard-working middle classes who have suffered most in recent years. It seemed as though the Government was determined to destroy this particular group.

Today, the frustration among the middle classes is almost palpable and definitely unbearable. Thousands feel angry, curiously alone and inexplicably afraid. Between a quarter and a third are talking, quite seriously, of emigrating.

Most of the middle classes are too sensible, too well-educated and too 'nice' to go out into the streets with placards. They won't throw stones at policemen or smash shop windows.

But it is from the middle classes that the revolution will come.

Throughout history, major protests, revolts, rebellions and revolutions have always come when the middle classes have been fed up with a rich, corrupt minority, with interests opposed to their own, making unreasonable demands and taking too much money.

Even Napoleon realised that the middle classes were the real revolutionaries. France has always been designed by its middle class revolutions.

158

'Nearly all the great popular revolts in England have taken place when the majority of working people, or at least a big section of them, were, or lately had been, doing fairly well. Then, suddenly, they have felt that attempts were being unjustly made to lower their standard of living or that of their class.'

HARRY ROBERTS

159

Throughout history the radical middle classes have been the only consistently reliable agents of social change.

It's worth a small detour into English history to prove that the middle classes can and do change things; a flashback into the history of reform and revolution the English way.

The Peasants' Revolt of 1381 was the first (and probably only spontaneous) English rebellion. At the time most people earned their living on the land.

In the middle of the 14th Century, the Black Death halved the population and the result was a labour shortage. Realising that they were in a good bargaining position labourers demanded, and were able to get, higher wages. And so in 1349, the King and Parliament (consisting of the barons) brought in the first Statute of Labourers which decreed that every person under the age of 60, who didn't have a trade, a craft or a master, had to work for whoever required him, at the wages which were 'customary before the visitation of the Great Plague'.

Any worker who refused to do this, or who threatened to go on strike, was liable to imprisonment. Any labourer refusing to work for pre-plague wages could be sent to prison for 15 days. Anyone taking a wage higher than the old wages was fined twice the sum taken.

Labourers were forbidden to change their employment without permission from their masters. And if a labourer left his parish, a writ for his recovery would be sent to every sheriff in England. If the labourer was caught he had the letter F burnt into his forehead. To make matters worse (and to maintain their income from a smaller population) the King and the barons introduced an unpopular poll tax.

This all caused some considerable upset and ill feeling but it didn't work. Wages were not kept down.

At the same time as honest working men were being stomped on by the 14th Century equivalent of the chattering classes, a man called John Wycliffe started to fight against the material prosperity of the church.

Monasteries had absorbed about a third of the land in England. Wycliffe protested and founded a new order of 'poor priests' who wore coarse brown wool clothes and moved around the country spreading Wycliffe's teaching that 'all men are equal' and that posh clergymen weren't entitled to live extravagantly while ordinary folk struggled to make ends meet. Wycliffe's followers were called Lollards.

The murmurings of protest grew louder. Rebels became cross that the King and his counsellors (or councillors) had grown rich at their expense. People complained, angrily, that public money was being wasted. Taxes were constantly being raised to pay for the court's extravagances. Services were deteriorating. The Magna Carta, though it had given rights to the people, and was a well-intentioned document, wasn't enough. These were the days of the original English superhero, Robin Hood.

Those involved in the Peasants' Revolt of the 14th Century were often illiterate and incapable of putting their feelings into words, but they were, nevertheless, conscious that they and their class were being treated unfairly.

The English rebels formed the Commons in Parliament, an assembly of outraged citizens which had no formal authority but which met simply to discuss taxes and other issues. The rebels allowed none of the King's counsellors into their Parliament. They elected a speaker and a Council of State. (There has been an office of speaker at the House of Commons since 1376. It has, until recently, been a position generally honoured by the holder and respected by all. The forced resignation of the speaker in 2009 was the first in over 300 years.)

This was the first stirring of English democracy. But the members of this early Parliament, although determined and searching for recognition, were not truly representative of the people and they had neither real power nor status. They sat for 74 days but when they finally dispersed and went home they left behind them no permanent organisation, no expectation of reassembling and no laws. Their views and wishes were quickly overturned by the expensively clad upper classes who had moats to clean and duck houses to pay for.

(It wasn't until several centuries later that a bloody civil war, a revolt of the middle classes against the twin powers of monarchy and church led by men such as Oliver Cromwell and John Lilburne, resulted in Parliament becoming the seat of power in England.)

The fact that their efforts had been pretty much in vain incensed the Lollards. One of Wycliffe's preachers was a chap called John Ball, also known as the 'crazy priest of Kent' (even then people who opposed the establishment were dismissed as lunatics).

Ball had three quarters of all the working men of eastern, middle and southern England behind him and despite being locked up three times he kept preaching.

Wyclifffe and Ball found support among tradesmen, craftsmen and artisans – the middle classes. New taxes lit the flames and led to a march on London. The leaders included Wat Tyler.

The demonstration in London was peaceful, though a few wild elements attacked rich men's homes and killed some lawyers and Government employees. No one much minded about the lawyers or the Government employees. The demonstrators even got away with destroying the palace of John of Gaunt, the hated uncle of the King and a principal minister.

Young King Richard II came to meet the protestors, agreed to their demands for freedom and promised to seal documents confirming this. But the next day Wat Tyler and the King got into a conversation and Tyler ended up quarrelling with the King's attendants who killed him. Naturally Tyler was falsely said to have attacked the King. This was early 'perception management' (now known as 'spin').

The mob got angry and the next day John Ball and another rebel called Jack Straw were caught and beheaded. Subsequently over 1,500 rebels were hung or beheaded. And so, technically the Peasants' Revolt was a failure. (It's known as the Peasants' Revolt but in those days the peasants were the equivalent of today's middle classes.)

However, within the next few decades everything the peasants had demanded was given. (This is nearly always what happens in effective rebellions.)

In 1450, the men of Kent rose up under a fellow called Jack Cade who used the nom de guerre John Mortimer. They were miffed about high taxes and rising prices and generally rotten conditions. Cade, or Mortimer, led 146,000 men, including many county gentlemen, squires and church ministers, and his army was able to defeat King Henry VI's army. After the match Cade's boys went to London, where they were welcomed and given the keys to the city.

Cade had regularly told his men that they should not steal – on pain of death – and though numerous oppressive ministers were beheaded (this was sensibly considered fair and reasonable) there was no stealing or looting.

Cade's rebellion led to the breakdown of royal authority in England.

160

'Be of good cheer, Master Ridley, for we have this day lit such a candle in England as shall, with God's grace, never be put out.'
BISHOP HUGH LATIMER ABOUT TO BE BURNT AT THE STAKE, COMFORTING AN OLD, WEAK MAN CALLED RIDLEY AS THE FAGGOTS UNDERNEATH THEM WERE LIT. LATIMER, ANOTHER MIDDLE CLASS REVOLUTIONARY WHO IS LARGELY FORGOTTEN, WAS BURNT IN 1555 FOR TREASON. DESPITE HIS ECCLESIASTICAL CONNECTIONS HE WAS A GOOD EGG AND HAD OPPOSED RENT RISES AND UNREASONABLE TAXES.

161

In the early part of the 19th Century, as a result of the industrial revolution and the Napoleonic wars, the rich were getting richer and the poor were getting poorer. Many felt it was necessary to get Parliament to amend the country's laws. Englishmen had seen how the French people had overthrown an unpopular government during the French revolution.

This was the time of William Cobbett, author and publisher. Cobbett was one of the greatest Englishmen of all time. He believed that England had a personality and that it needed and deserved a genuine 'England' policy. He believed it was important to preserve the personal peculiar characteristics of England and to respect the special individual liberties enshrined in the nation's history and culture. He believed that a popularly elected Parliament, representing an informed democracy, would end the borough mongering and the sinecures which still disgraced public life. Naturally, Cobbett wasn't popular with the boys with the moats and the duck houses. He was imprisoned for defending freedom and the rights of ordinary working men.

162

'By God's grace we will recover the liberties of our country - not by violence, anarchy or brute force, but by the peaceful, organised and magnificent display of the will of the people. When the barons of Runnymede recovered the liberties of England from the tyrant John, they took up the bow, and the spear, and the battle-axe, and the sword, and they were justified in so doing. Thank God, we have no occasion now to take up murderous and destructive weapons like these; the progress of education and knowledge has changed this state of things; our weapons are truth, justice and reason; our sword is the 'sword of the spirit' which is the will of the people, and let no one doubt that this great moral sword is efficient for every just and useful purpose.'

THOMAS ATTWOOD, A BANKER, A MIDDLE CLASS REVOLUTIONARY AND A SUPPORTER OF PARLIAMENTARY REFORM, SPEAKING AT THE BIRMINGHAM UNION IN 1830.

163

Two weeks after Attwood's speech, on the opening day of Parliament, the Prime Minister, the Duke of Wellington, sniffily stated that he was not prepared to introduce any reforms.

Thirteen days after that Wellington's Government was defeated and the Iron Duke resigned. So, yah boo sucks to Wellington. He might have defeated Napoleon but the middle classes were too much for him.

The new Prime Minister was Earl Grey, a member of 'The Friends of the People', a society which wanted reform of parliamentary representation. Meetings had been held all over the country and many messages of support and encouragement had been sent to Lord Grey.

Grey didn't find it easy but eventually he won. The Reform Bill was introduced into the House of Commons in March 1831 and finally passed in June 1832.

Sadly, although this bill enfranchised the well-to-do commercial classes, the lower middle class and working class wage earners still had no vote. In that respect the bill turned out to be a disappointment. Social conditions were subsequently allowed to deteriorate so much that the workhouses and debtors' prisons immortalised by Charles Dickens became a part of English society. Not surprisingly, the lower middle classes felt disappointed and let down.

In 1836, William Lovett founded a society called the London Working Men's Association. The society, aimed at artisans who had been ignored in the Reform Bill, drew up the People's Charter (which was actually written by a tailor called Francis Place). As a result, its members were known as Chartists. Their campaigning eventually gave them the parliamentary representation they wanted.

164

'You must become your own social and political regenerators, or you will never enjoy freedom. For true liberty cannot be conferred by Acts of Parliament or decrees of princes, but must spring up from the knowledge,

morality and public virtue of our population…Though revolution were
to follow revolution, and changes were to be continually effected in
our constitution, laws and government, unless the social and political
superstructure were based upon the intelligence and morality of the
people, they would only have exchanged despotism for despotism,
and one set of oppressors for another.'

WILLIAM LOVETT, CABINET MAKER AND REVOLUTIONARY.

165

The Fabian Society (named after Roman general Fabius Cunctator whose tactics the society decided to adopt) was founded in 1884 and early members included Sidney Webb, Annie Besant and the Irishman George Bernard Shaw. Their basic aim was to persuade the English people to make their political constitution thoroughly democratic. They produced pamphlets, gave lectures and influenced social legislation in England for the remains of the 19th Century and the early part of the 20th Century.

166

It is interesting to note that most of the rebellions and nearly all the reforms which occurred in English history were backed by individuals who were not themselves suffering from the grievances they worked to remove. This is true philanthropy (not the modern kind, which involves a tax dodge, a publicity stunt and a cheque which never actually arrives).

So, among England's greatest reformers were William Wilberforce, John Howard, Elizabeth Fry and Florence Nightingale. Their reforms changed the world, not just England, and they all relied upon changing public opinion to produce change.

Other revolutionaries worth remembering include philosopher John Stuart Mill, who campaigned for women's' rights long before the bra was invented let alone being burnt, and Mary Wollstonecraft, who was campaigning for votes for women long before Mrs Pankhurst started chaining herself to things. Mary Wollstonecraft published *A Vindication of the Rights of Women* in 1792.

Revolutionary social ideas were popularised by great artists such as Milton in the 17th Century, Blake and Shelley in the early part of the 19th Century and, in the later part of the century, John Ruskin and William Morris.

167

Nearly all the victories won by rebels in England have been achieved without a blow being struck (if you ignore the occasional beheading of some snotty Sheriff of Nottingham type). Change occurred because those in power (the ruling minority) realised that they were in a weak and ultimately indefensible position.

We can learn three things about reform and revolution from our history:

1. Reform always begins with dissent among the middle classes. Revolution never comes from high above. The aristocracy and the ruling classes have no need to revolt and nothing to revolt against. And revolution never comes from the bottom tiers of society. Revolt, and subsequently reform, always begins with the people who are, and always have been, the backbone of English society: the hard-working middle classes. And revolt starts when the middle classes feel aggrieved because they are being used and abused and taken advantage of by self-indulgent leaders.

2. When the middle classes revolt there may be violence - resulting either from the actions of a small group of hot-headed demonstrators or, more likely, the actions of those employed to protect and defend the oppressive ruling class. But it is not the violence which produces change. It is the meetings and the independent publication of books and pamphlets which really produces long-term, substantial change. The change occurs because the meetings are attended by large numbers of protestors and the books and pamphlets are read by large numbers of people. Change occurs when dissent spreads.

3. There is always a delay between the substantial call for change and the change itself. The ruling classes always struggle to resist the inevitable but eventually they bow to it because it

is inevitable. The longer reform is delayed the bloodier the consequences for the establishment. Refusals to act lead to extended periods of chaos.

168

The problem today is simpler and easier to solve than at any time in our history. As I have been arguing for years, our problem is caused by the power of the political parties. It is time to get rid of them. And let us not make the mistake of replacing the big three parties with smaller political parties.

We need to take this opportunity to rid ourselves of all political parties. We never needed them. We do not need them now. And we will never benefit from their presence.

169

Since Labour came to power in 1997 the English have handed over nearly £1.5 trillion in income tax. They've handed over container loads more in VAT, business taxes, death duties, stamp duties, fuel surcharges and so on. The English middle classes have been robbed blind, deaf and dumb.

Taxes have soared and services have deteriorated daily. Family life has been debased by a system that gives generous handouts to asylum seekers and encourages pregnancy among teenage girls.

The Government showed that it cared only about the scroungers (who provide the votes to keep their party in power) and the greedy MPs (who act as lobby fodder and a substitute for democracy).

170

Blair and Brown, two Scottish invaders, rose to power entirely through the political party system. They got there partly through their own absurdly inflated self-belief and partly because of the English way of refusing to say anything critical of boorish guests.

We put up with them because we are all too polite and well-mannered and, well, too damned nice.

Well, bugger niceness. We've been silent hosts for far too long. It is politeness, and not liking to speak up for fear of offending someone, that has got us into this mess.

171

It used to be said that if you were polite to people in authority (policemen, customs officers and officials from the council) and had nothing to hide or to worry about then they would talk to you politely, listen to you, tip their hats and go on their way.

That may have been true a few decades ago. It is certainly not true now.

172

Politicians used to dismiss anyone who questioned the sanctity of our Government as nutters. These days they are more likely to dismiss critics as terrorists or terrorist supporters. Anyone who dares to question what is happening is marginalised. Anyone who dares to question the three main parties is regarded as a dangerous heretic. The three main parties are, of course, now so indistinguishable from one another that if you criticise one you criticise them all.

The Government has even done its best to ban political parties whose views it doesn't like. And you can't get much more fascist than that.

173

Ministers who want to ban political parties such as the British National Party, either don't realise or don't care that banning membership of a political party would be a clear breach of the Human Rights Act.

Article 10 (entitled Freedom of Expression) states quite clearly: 'You have the right to hold opinions and express your views on your own or in a group. This applies even if they are unpopular or disturbing. This right can only be restricted in specified circumstances (such as protecting the public health or safety, preventing crime and protecting the rights of others).'

174

Writing and reading are regarded as subversive acts because the very actions of writing and reading question the idea that things have to be the way they are. Moreover, they destroy the idea that you are alone in thinking the way you do.

175

Millions think the same because no one really thinks. Anyone who questions the accepted 'truths', and dares to think outside the box, is immediately branded a dangerous heretic, a traitor, a terrorist.

176

Everything is forbidden unless it is expressly allowed.

177

The establishment (the Westminster village of MPs, lobbyists, political correspondents and commentators) closes ranks to exclude any danger to its cosy, self-satisfied sense of security.

Politicians from different parties pretend to shout at one another, but when the curtain goes down they all repair to the bar and have a heavily subsidised snifter together.

178

The Government, supported and egged on by some pretty rancid journalists and commentators, has been fighting a war on thrift, prudence, marriage, hard work, honesty, loyalty, respect, responsibility and integrity – just about everything once described as 'middle class values'.

Politicians regularly sneer at the middle classes and the very values which made England great.

In their place the sneerers have given us multiculturalism, political-correctness, targets and means-testing: the four horsemen of our Apocalypse.

179

Under the auspices of the party system, we have become a nation of special interests, all represented by skilful lobbyists and all demanding a bigger and bigger slice of the communal tax cake.

The people who do all the work, and who are the engine room of our nation, the working middle class (the people who provide the wealth which the special interest groups enjoy) are derided and scorned and ignored.

It cannot continue.

180

It is hardly surprising that several hundred thousand hard working people leave England every year, in search of a fairer society where, ideally, their virtues and hard work may stand a chance of being acknowledged and where, at the very least, they can escape from the sneering, the grasping and the oppression.

In May 2009, a writer in *The Sun* newspaper encouraged young families to desert Britain and head for Australia or New Zealand and a new life.

Survey after survey has shown that between a quarter and a third of hard-working, tax-paying Englishmen and women are seriously planning to emigrate.

Politicians say they do not care.

They should. Oh, how they should.

181

We need to find a way to say: 'Here I am. This is what I stand for. This is the sort of country I believe we need. I've taken enough abuse, manipulation and deceit. I'm fed up with greedy, incompetent people running the country for their own benefit rather than for the benefit of the nation and our communities.'

We need to find a new way to say it because the politicians have consistently failed to listen to us.

182

As a nation we have lost our way. But there is a way forward; there is a way in which we can survive the damage done by our politicians.

We need to think outside the box. We need to use our minds and our imaginations to find a simple solution that will work.

There is a way; but there is only one way.

Politicians and bureaucrats will never downsize Government, any more than they will repeal laws or hand back power.

Today, the three parties, and the bureaucratic machinery they control, are our enemy.

They, and the EU, are a far, far greater and more consistent threat to our future than any terrorist group on earth.

To paraphrase George W. Bush, the politicians are either with us (the people) or they are against us. They are with us or they are the enemy.

They are certainly not with us. And so they are the enemy.

The party system has failed miserably to provide leadership or good management.

183

Great things happen only through the work of unreasonable men. Only when enough unreasonable men come together to work for the public good is society changed for the better.

184

Many people have pretty well given up. They no longer believe that it is, or ever will be, possible to change anything.

It looks like communal apathy and lethargy but in fact it's worse than that: its communal depression.

Instead of protesting ('What's the point?') the millions who do the work which pays for the politicians, the bureaucrats, the regulators, the airport Gestapo and all the rest of it just put their heads down and work ever harder in order to pay their ever increasing taxes.

They try not to notice that most of the money they contribute is wasted. They try not to notice that, despite the ever-rising taxes, the nation's infrastructure is crumbling and that if they want half way decent health care, or half way decent education for their children, they must pay extra for it.

They live, as Thoreau wrote, lives of quiet desperation. And they escape into alcohol and television.

Many people have had their spirit broken by unjust laws, overzealous regulations and a vast army of bureaucrats.

185

'Good men must not obey the laws too well.'
RALPH WALDO EMERSON

186

All our liberties are due to men who, when their conscience has compelled them, have broken the laws of the land.

187

The green shoots of a revolution are appearing.

I don't mean a guns and barricades sort of revolution.

Even if that was our way, which it is not, that sort of revolution would be squashed within hours by Government hired thugs using guns and chemical weapons. (All paid for by the people protesting, of course.)

I mean a bloodless revolution.

All over England, thousands of angry citizens are reading, talking, listening and spreading the word. The number who realise that our current system is indefensible and unsustainable is growing rapidly.

A few years ago, in my first political book, *England Our England*, I wrote: 'we want our country back'. And that's exactly what thousands are now saying.

We want our country back. We want an end to injustice. We want to be respected and treated as citizens, not slaves. We want our taxes to be spent wisely and discriminately. We want an end to open door immigration policies. We want to leave the European Union. We want an end to political correctness, an end to means-testing, an end to pointless targets, an end to multiculturalism, an end to positive discrimination (punishing the white middle classes for the sins of another age) and an end to the loss of our rights in some misguided, misplaced, manipulated 'war on terror'.

We want an efficient, lean Government that provides a basic infrastructure that works and a simple, system of nation management that is fair and just.

We want an end to waste and arms profiteering. We want our leaders to offer us moral guidance not petty, niggling rules and regulations designed to keep us in our place.

188

Our society is not working.

We do not need such a complex society. Smaller and simpler really would be better and beautiful. We need to go back to basics; we need to understand what we need from our Government. And then we have to decide how best we can achieve that.

The State has failed its employers (us) and would have been fired in disgrace if it had been a normal employee.

We don't want tinkering with the system. We want big changes – big changes that none of the three main political parties is offering or is ever going to offer.

189

People who dare to protest about what is happening are always told that if they feel strongly about something they should write letters to their Parliamentary representative.

Fat lot of good that will do.

We are told that we have the power of the ballot box.

But which party do you vote for if you want to leave the EU, stop starting wars or get rid of laws restricting our freedom?

There is no choice.

None of the three main parties is of any use to us. Supporters of the 'party' system, say that there is no need for people to go on the streets or to write letters of protest.

'We live in a parliamentary democracy,' they claim sniffily. 'If you are dissatisfied with some aspect of our society then you should use the ballot box to make your views known.'

Oh yeah?

And just how will that help?

Who do we vote for to get what we really need?

There is no democracy. There is no democratic process.

The political parties are all the same. There are no real political choices.

190

But the ballot box can be our weapon if we use it properly and wisely: and it is a weapon that we must use now before they remove it.

We can use the ballot box to get precisely what we want: quickly, easily and without bloodshed.

We can use the ballot box to win the bloodless revolution.

A bloodless revolution that will succeed in just one day.

191

There are many arguments for doing nothing and we have been listening to them for years.

We should not have been so patient or so complacent or so compliant.

Some have argued that there is no point in doing anything because we cannot change things. Others have suggested that the Government, and the system, will collapse under its own weight of immorality.

Many more have pointed out, justifiably, that anyone who sticks his or her head above the parapet is likely to have it shot off.

We wonder still how the German people allowed Hitler and the strutting Nazis to get so much power, stay in power and do so much harm. But I believe we have allowed Blair and Brown to do far more long-term harm to England than Hitler did to England or Germany.

Scottish politicians will lead us into despair, through stubbornness and into revolution.

The bottom line is that if we don't respect ourselves, and defend our honour, we can hardly expect anyone else to respect us.

192

One thing, and only one thing, is certain beyond dispute. England is in for a terrible future. The debt created by Gordon Brown (and which he was allowed to accumulate by the other two leading parties) has ruined England for generations to come. It will take generations to recover from the economic and social chaos created by a decade of appalling mismanagement. Taxes will rise, rise and rise again. And services will deteriorate beyond the gloomiest fears of those providing and those receiving. The on-going crisis created by Brown's incompetence (and, in the fullness of time, Brown will be seen as such an incompetent manager of the nation's finances that the worst of the banking dross, the Fred Goodwins, will be remembered as acceptably, almost whimsically flawed) will merge with two coming crises: the soaring oil price, resulting from the consequences of peak oil, and the increasing dependency of an ageing and disabled population, a problem which has been accelerated by the dramatic increase in emigration resulting from Brown's policies and the widening of the definition of 'disabled' and 'incapable'.

We need sound, honest, good men and women at the nation's head. And we must neither expect too much of them nor expect them to take on more responsibility than they can handle comfortably.

It has long been assumed that great emergencies produce men competent to deal with them. The Second World War gave us Churchill. But the failure of the Crash of 2007 to produce anyone closely resembling a leader gives the lie to that age-old assumption.

We must adapt our political processes, rather than await the arrival of a saviour.

193

The party system has grown to be so powerful that no strong-minded, honest, *independent* individual can thrive in politics. In order to succeed in party politics (and to reach a position of authority and power within a political party) an individual must be able to suppress his own passions, and to replace honestly held views with convenient compromises. To succeed within a modern political party a politician must be prepared to deceive and to lie.

Party politics is the art of compromise and is therefore an anathema to anyone with real convictions or any sense of responsibility or commitment. You can't compromise if you have ethical standards so by definition politicians don't have ethical standards.

Parties require politicians to lie and to support ideas and policies of which they do not approve. Most honest politicians, when pressed, will admit they spend much of their careers espousing policies with which they do not agree.

Those are the skills which lead to success within a party system. But are they really the skills we want in our politicians?

I believe not.

194

As I have already mentioned, millions of people have decided that the only answer is to leave the country. Millions of hard working, middle class English families have left England to seek new lives abroad. Millions more are planning to follow them. Scroungers don't emigrate. They're happy to stay.

The Government doesn't care. It is happy to see free-thinking, independent-minded citizens leave the country. (It will care when it realises that the people who have been paying for the party have left, and that there is no one left to pay the bills.)

But is emigration really the only answer for those of us who care?

I don't believe so.

There is one thing (a very simple thing) that we can do that will make a difference and that will enable us to reclaim our nation. It won't cost us a penny. It won't take more than a few minutes of our time. And it is guaranteed to work.

195

'Another hindrance to civilisation today is the over-organisation of our public life. While it is certain that a properly ordered environment is the condition and, at the same time, the result of civilisation, it is also undeniable that, after a certain point has been reached, external organisation is developed at the expense of spiritual life. Personality and ideas are often subordinated to institutions, when it is really these which ought to influence the latter and keep them inwardly alive.'

DR ALBERT SCHWEIZER

196

Politicians do not own the country, or control us, any more than the police are our masters. And once in every century or so there comes an opportunity to remind them of that, and to seek a real change in the way we run our country, an opportunity to show that it is our country and that it is up to us to decide how we want it run.

In the 20th Century two attempts were made to change the nature of the State. The first was crucial and ultimately destructive. The second involved tinkering at the edges rather than fundamental change.

The first change took place in the late 1940s, after years of poverty and war, when the Labour Party decided to build a Welfare State with free health care and benefits for all. It was England's first experiment in statism. It sounded wonderful. It proved to be a disaster.

After thirty years, when it became clear that Labour's ambitious experiment was failing miserably, and that the State was taking over too much of our lives, Margaret Thatcher's Government, tried to limit the extent of the State. That was the second attempt to change the State.

Thatcher failed, of course.

She talked about 'rolling back the frontiers of the State' and made real efforts to take the Government out of the management of steel, coal, car production and the utilities. The problem was that she was restrained by two things: the bureaucrats and the power of the voters who relied upon the State for their income.

Making cuts in any large bureaucracy is difficult because the bureaucrats who work for it are committed first and foremost to keeping their jobs, their power and their status. They do not want to relinquish any of these delights. If costs have to be cut then they will be made on the front line. People doing the real work will be laid off. Services will be cut. But administrators remain in their jobs.

And so England now has a pathetic infrastructure, but a massive bureaucracy.

Thatcher didn't just have to contend with the bureaucrats. She also had to deal with the fact that millions of people had become addicted to the Welfare State and did not want it dismantling. If anything, they wanted it to be made bigger. By the 1970s, the Welfare State was soaking up about two thirds of all Government spending. And the people benefiting from all that money (the State bureaucrats and those receiving State benefits) didn't want things to change. Between them they had enough votes to make sure that nothing did change.

Worse still, Thatcher took us deeper into the European Union, and gave us another layer of bureaucracy.

Sadly, her well-intentioned tinkering made things worse. She was not brave enough, or imaginative enough, to bring about the real changes that were needed.

197

All politicians who want to change things are constrained by the party system, whereby the only parliamentary candidates who are likely to be successful are the ones sponsored by, and controlled by, political parties.

This means that there is no room for independent, original thinking – either in the leadership or within the body of the party.

The only politicians who are successful are the ones who are prepared to put the party first and the electorate and the nation joint second. (Actually, the electorate and the nation come a distant joint third. They put themselves second.)

The three political parties long ago moved away from representing the people and into the business of looking after their own interests.

They have become corporate beasts with agendas of their own. Political parties exist to look after themselves, and to further their own power, and not to protect or serve the country. Their interests, and the country's interests are permanently, diametrically opposed.

We are innocent victims of the three party trick.

198

The disastrous years of Blair and Brown have weakened England so much that we now need real, imaginative changes. The power must be put back into the hands of the people to whom the country belongs.

The Labour Governments which have run the country since 1997 have been racist (in that money has been taken out of England and given to Scotland in order to sustain the Labour Party there) and fascist (in that they have given increasing amounts of power to the most fascist organisation ever invented, the European Union).

It's now too late for tinkering.

If we don't do something to redesign our future then whether the Labour Party or the Conservative Party manage our future, the economic disaster created by Brown and others will result in severe social unrest, massively higher taxes, dramatically reduced public services, an ever more crumbling infrastructure, more social interventions, worsening race relations, more control for institutions such as the European Union and the International Monetary Fund, more statism, civil war and the rapid end of England as an independent nation.

You may think I'm exaggerating.

But I should warn you that everything else I've predicted in my previous books has come true.

We need change; real change, not tinkering.

199

The institutions, the politicians and the civil servants we have trusted with the management of our world are, in that modern jargon, 'not fit for purpose'. They have failed miserably. Worse, they have cheated us and taken advantage of our trust.

We must take back the power which is rightfully ours.

200

'Dull apathy and smug complacency seemed to be about to bring the British Empire tottering to its knees, if it didn't knock it out altogether.'
WING COMMANDER GUY GIBSON VC DSO DFC
LEADER OF THE DAM BUSTERS RAID IN THE SECOND WORLD WAR

201

All over the world the party system has enabled corrupt politicians to obtain power and to hold onto it. Today's politicians can be bought for a two week holiday in a nice villa, the chance to mix with celebrities and the promise of a well-paid company directorship. No corrupt independent politician could ever win or retain power in the way that corrupt party politicians can do. Think of a corrupt politician anywhere in the world and there will, behind him or her, be a corrupt party.

Modern party politicians are utterly lacking in responsibility or any sense of respect or decency. They are driven by arrogance and self regard.

The party system gives authority and power to the sycophantic in preference to the independent and creative. Politicians who have never done anything more expensive than buy a house (a purchase requiring a few hundred thousand pounds) suddenly find themselves playing with vast amounts of public money and having the authority to approve purchases costing hundreds of millions.

202

The Labour Years which started in 1997 will go down in history as the most corrupt in English history.

The party created a culture of excess during which the greedy few, working in financial institutions and large companies and for the Government and the public sector, enriched themselves at the expense of the poor and the middle classes.

In a fair world, a dozen ministers and several hundred back bench MPs would be in prison, serving sentences for war crimes, fraud or theft. Politicians have had things their own way for long enough.

203

Gordon Brown, destroyer and wastrel and the architect of England's demise, had a long history of friendship with financiers. His campaign for leadership of the party was, for example, supported by a private equity industry millionaire.

Would Brown have created an overpriced, massively flawed and astonishingly incompetent regulatory system, or devised economic and political policies which helped create and then sustain the climate of greed if he had not been so close to such folk?

It is an undeniable fact that if Brown had not been a member of a political party he would not have needed to campaign for the leadership of that party and he would not have needed to raise money for his campaign.

204

Today, there are no significant differences between the three main parties. You couldn't slide a sheet of greaseproof paper between their policies and so, effectively, we live in a one party state. The big three parties have given us consensus politics – stuff no one believes in. The people who would make the best politicians, honest people who really care about the world they live in and who are honest and passionate, are excluded from the political process because they do not, and never would, fit into the all-powerful but utterly discredited party system.

205

The big three political parties don't exist to protect England or, indeed, to defend or protect the voters. The three political parties in England exist to defend themselves. It is the parties which set the agendas and dictate the terms of engagement.

The politicians who are members of those parties, who are naive enough to think that they are in Parliament to promote themselves and their own interests, are, in reality, in Parliament to promote and preserve the interests of their party.

206

We have moved seamlessly from a Parliament of parties representing royalists and cavaliers to a Parliament representing conservative, labour and liberal parties. Political parties are served by power-hungry people who are always scheming to deceive the public and to maintain their party's position. Individual party MPs are bought and paid for with appointments, money and status; their loyalty remains always to the party machine rather than to their constituents.

The party system has given us unending government by liars, cheats, hypocrites, incompetents and self-serving buffoons. Party politicians are driven solely by a desire for instant popularity because it is that which leads to electoral success for their party. They have no care for the long-term good of the nation.

Political parties are essentially all about compromise. Those who represent them can never be men or women of firm convictions; they are inevitably weak creatures who will change their views to fit in with the party's needs.

It is hardly surprising that, for all practical purposes, our nation has become a one party state.

207

Many people would like to stop subsidising the arms industry, and to stop selling arms to countries which are (or may become) our enemies.

But the Labour Government, the most warmongering Government Britain has ever had, gave £890 million of taxpayers' money a year to the British arms industry. As a result of this generosity Britain became the world's biggest arms seller with an arms industry accounting for a third of global arms exports.

The Government actually has an organisation (the Defence Export Service Organisation) which exists solely to market and sell UK arms. Through this organisation British taxpayers promote arms fairs organised to drum up interest in new ways of killing and wounding people. It is, of course, impossible to prove this but I have been told by a military source that the British army was kept active in Northern Ireland for longer than necessary so that the Government could sell arms 'as tested in an urban context'.

Why does the Government do this? Simple. It's a vote winner. Subsidising the arms industry helps sustain the Labour party.

Political parties need to win several hundred parliamentary seats in order to win an election and form a Government. And giving money to the arms industry helps political parties win seats, win elections and gain power.

The result of the subsidy is that each job in the arms industry costs UK taxpayers over £13,000 a year. Taxpayers are subsidising the manufacture and sale of bombs, landmines and other weapons of mass destruction.

With an arms industry to maintain it is, perhaps, not surprising that politicians from all sides have, in recent years, been extremely slow to criticise foreign countries which have policies which the people of Britain find repugnant.

On the contrary, our Governments have sold arms to regimes which most people in Britain would describe as cruel and oppressive.

208

According to Parliament's own website the seven principles of public office are: selflessness, integrity, objectivity, accountability, openness, honesty and leadership. Can you name a single holder of public office who represents any of those virtues – let alone all of them? And which of them do our current leaders display?

If we get the leaders we deserve then we have to believe that we deserve our current batch of politicians. And that simply isn't believable. We don't deserve such people. And so there must be something seriously and intrinsically wrong with the system. And the something is the way that the three main political parties have taken over Parliament.

The party system encourages betrayal and attracts self-serving individuals. We need to get rid of our existing party political system and start again – from scratch.

209

'I believe there will ultimately be a clash between the oppressed and those who do the oppressing. I believe there will be a clash between those who want freedom, justice and equality for everyone, and those who want to continue the system of exploitation. I believe there will be that kind of clash, but I don't think it will be based on the colour of the skin.'
MALCOLM X (1925–1965)

210

The members of our modern political parties never question accepted or acknowledged truths. No one thinks outside the box. They are prejudiced, selfish and blind to injustice. They regard some elements of political life, such as the existence of the National Health Service and our membership of the European Union, as beyond debate.

It is widely agreed by those working for it that the NHS has failed. But politicians never dream of contemplating alternatives.

The majority of citizens in England want to quit the European Union but none of the three main political parties offer that option at elections.

The big issues are always ignored and the voters' attention distracted with insignificant side-issues or manufactured crises and threats.

Think of half a dozen recent politicians. Pick any half dozen you like. Write down their names.

Any voting system which gives power to people like those is clearly not working. Any country which persists with such a system is doomed and deserves to be.

We want and need politicians with wisdom, sincerity and passion. We want and need politicians who care about others as much as they care about themselves. We want and need politicians for whom the word 'community' has real meaning.

211

Because the party system has to provide secure employment for as many of its supporters as possible we have far too many MPs. Much larger countries (America, for example) manage with far fewer political representatives. Even though most of our legislation comes from Brussels and is created by unelected bureaucrats in Brussels, the House of Commons has 646 MPs for a population of 60 million. India has a population of 1.1 billion and 545 members of its Parliament. The USA, with a population of 300 million has 435 members in its House of Representatives.

212

Today's party system means that MPs are given 'safe' parliamentary seats in reward for services rendered to the party. They then return the favour by voting according to the requirements of the party leaders who put them there, rather than in the interests of the people who voted for them. Their primary loyalties are always to the party and never to the country or the constituents.

Today, most MPs have never done any other work and know nothing of the real world outside one of the three political parties. Many are given their seats as a reward for sucking up to a sitting, powerful politician. These ladder-climbing nonentities, an army of dedicated liars and thieves, will do whatever they are told to do. If they are told to vote for war, they will vote for war. If they are told to hand over our country to the European Union they will do that too. In the House of Commons, members of Parliament stream into the voting lobbies asking one another 'Which way am I supposed to be voting on this?' They have little or no real interest in the legislation being passed. Our modern political structures have become barriers to democracy.

The country is run by a consortium of thieves and liars. (By which I do not mean two groups of people, some of whom are thieves and some of whom are liars, but one group of people who are both thieves and liars.)

213

People vote for political parties regardless of the skills, qualities or honesty of their local candidates. It is this that has led to the election of so many petty crooks. We need to get back to a world wherein voters choose the candidate not the party.

214

Ministers used to take responsibility for their actions and for the actions of those working in their departments. No more. Modern ministers have no sense of honour or shame. Modern politicians lie and steal and fiddle their expenses but rarely consider resigning. There is no dignity. No one in public service (either as a politician or a civil servant) ever admits to making a mistake or doing something wrong. England has become like a banana republic in many senses but especially in the fact that the population now always assumes that they are being lied to whenever a Government minister speaks. No one who wasn't dropped on their head at birth believes the 'official' version any more. Everything is spun (which is the modern word for self-preserving lying). Politicians lie so much that no one knows, or takes any notice, when they do tell the truth. They have cried 'wolf' so many times that they are no longer believed. Modern governments are packed with slick confidence tricksters. No one trusts them; no one believes what they say; their reassurances and exhortations fall on stony ground.

215

Politicians are out of touch with the will of the electorate who put them in power. They are out of touch with the people's will because they are out of touch with the people. After a few months in office ministers begin to believe that they are in power because they are superior; they are bowed to by civil servants because they are 'special'; they are driven around in chauffeur driven limousines because they are 'special'; they are protected by armed policemen because they are 'special'.

They believe they are in politics not to improve the lot of the electorate but to indulge themselves.

The country is run on a mixture of prejudice, expediency and self-interest and the party system (which provides 99% of our MPs) is built on compromise born of greed.

Men and women who are willing to toe the party line and creep and crawl their way through the election process (being careful never to express any personal opinions or upset any of the colourless characters whose votes they need) are the only ones to succeed. The whole electoral process is controlled by the subhuman riff-raff who choose the local party candidates. And the only skill that takes a candidate through that process is deceit: the ability to mask whatever they might be thinking and to deceive the committee, their colleagues, the voters and the party hierarchy.

The greater your capacity for deceit the greater your future in British politics.

What have we done?

216

'A nation can survive its fools, and even the ambitious. But it cannot survive treason from within. An enemy at the gates is less formidable, for he is known and he carries his banners openly. But the traitor moves among those within the gate freely, his sly whispers rustling through all the alleys, heard in the very halls of government itself. For the traitor appears no traitor; he speaks in the accents familiar to his victims, and he wears their face and their garments, and he appeals to the baseness that lies deep in the hearts of all men. He rots the soul of a nation; he works secretly and unknown in the night to undermine the pillars of a city; he infects the body politic so that it can no longer resist. A murderer is less to be feared.'
MARCUS TULLIUS CICERO

217

In the 19th Century, Parliament was devalued by the existence of 'rotten boroughs'. Ambitious but pliant young sycophants were given a seat in Parliament in exchange for promising to vote according to the wishes of their sponsor – the owner of the 'rotten borough'. The owner of the 'rotten borough' controlled the votes and made sure (by bribery or violence or a mixture of both) that there was no serious competition.

What is the difference between a rotten borough of the 19th Century and a parliamentary constituency of the 21st Century, where an ambitious but pliant young sycophant is given a safe seat as approved by a parliamentary party which has, through bullying, guile and trickery acquired virtual ownership of the seat?

The big three political parties have given themselves huge advantages over independent candidates (free television advertising is the most obvious) and they do their best to make things expensive and difficult for the honest, principled candidate.

What's the difference between the rotten boroughs of the 19th Century and the way that Scottish politicians are allowed to vote on issues that affect only English citizens? They do so under instruction from their party leaders, just as the holders of 'rotten borough' seats voted as instructed by the local land owner who owned their seat and their vote?

The truth, of course, is that there is no difference. The wishes and needs of the ordinary citizen are ignored. The sponsor or benefactor who, through inheritance, owned a 'rotten borough' was no more or less democratic than the representatives of the modern parliamentary parties. In each case the MP votes as he is told to vote, ignoring his obligations to the electorate.

218

Charging huge fees from those who want to stand for Parliament as independent candidates helps to protect the party system. The party system helps to preserve the State and so the State helps to preserve the party system.

Anyone not in one of the main parties is dismissed by the

various strands of the establishment as a 'nutter' whose views (whatever they might be) are not to be taken seriously.

Ensuring that publicity is given only to the big political parties which support the system (and the State) ensures that small parties have no chance of success.

219

The tragedy today, and the reason for many of our problems, is that the great majority of politicians have never done anything else for a living – and cannot and could not do anything to earn their daily bread. They are, almost by definition, vain and ambitious. Their reliance on politics as a means of earning a living means that they will do anything – including lie and deceive – to hang onto office. Only when the lies run out do they resign. Honour is, to them, an unaffordable luxury. Modern politicians don't resign on principle, partly because they have no principles but also because there is nothing else they can do.

This is the fault of the party system.

Political parties need to attract and then appoint parliamentary candidates who will do as they are told and who will vote the way they are told to vote. The last thing political parties want is a Parliament filled with independent, passionate, ethical MPs.

220

Modern politicians never stand up for unpopular causes – even if they believe in them. Their policies are ruled by political correctness rather than passion. Every penny they've ever earned has usually come from taxpayers via the Government. They enjoy an entirely misplaced sense of moral and intellectual superiority.

Wherever nations are ruled by party politics the same is true.

It's hardly surprising that professional party politicians all over the world are in prison, in court or on the run. There's barely a country on the planet which doesn't have (or hasn't recently had) an unpleasant rash of crooked politicians.

221

Most of our politicians have no real life experience. Most have never had to deal with the real problems which face entrepreneurs and businessmen and so they have no idea what effort is required and energy wasted, in wading through the red tape they have helped create.

Modern MPs have no understanding of, or concern for, the unreasonable challenges they have placed in the way of creative working people – the people upon whose shoulders a nation's present and future always depends.

Our world is run by people who may be formally educated but who have never learned to question what they have been told and have no valid life experience with which to create judgements. It is not surprising that they believe they can solve all problems if they pass enough laws, create enough red tape and devise enough crude social engineering programmes.

Inevitably, the average citizen has less respect for politicians than any other professional group other than lawyers.

Is it merely a coincidence that most politicians were trained as lawyers?

222

Up until 1911, MPs were paid nothing. Serving as an MP was seen as a privilege and a duty. MPs often had other jobs (running farms and businesses or working as barristers, doctors, journalists or union officials) and sat in the House of Commons as true representatives of the people they knew and worked alongside. Gladstone and Disraeli had no need of expenses or research assistants. MPs would have been insulted if they had been offered a salary.

223

In order to ensure a better quality of politician we should elect only older MPs. It is utterly absurd that there should be men and women sitting in the House of Commons who are not out of their twenties. No one under the age of 40 should be eligible to be elected to Parliament.

Parliament is stuffed with young and inexperienced MPs because it's a lot easier to push around a 25-year-old with no experience and no money than it is to push around a 65-year-old who has a lifetime's experience and enough money to live on.

224

"The State' may come to mean no more than a self-elected political party; and oligarchy and privilege can return, based on power rather than on money.'
GEORGE ORWELL

225

Throughout the scandal over MPs expenses in 2009, the Government talked much and often about finding a solution. Committees were set up. Experts were consulted.

It would have surely taken a fairly ordinary corporate accountant no more than one hour to replace the nonsensical system in place with a system designed to be fair to MPs and to taxpayers.

The failure of the Government to take such simple action showed that there was no political will to replace a system that had caused massive public distrust and dissatisfaction. Dissent and dissatisfaction rumbled on until, in June 2009, a poll showed that over half the country thought that all MPs were corrupt. You can't run a country with a government which is regarded with such contempt and loathing.

226

Are our MPs inherently bad people?

Some undoubtedly are, and some are simply misguided; too vain and greedy to resist temptation when it appears. But to be honest it really doesn't matter a damn because the problem lies really in the party system.

The party system encourages corruption, injustice and a self-serving attitude which pervades everything.

Remember: political parties have no interest in people or countries. They exist solely to sustain and strengthen themselves.

227

In return for their obedience to the party, modern politicians are paid fat salaries. And expenses. Lots and lots of expenses.

Half a century ago MPs took no expenses at all except a pittance for the cost of postage. But in 1957, MPs voted to allow themselves a parliamentary allowance of £750 to cover basic costs. That was the opening of the floodgates.

228

Today, almost a third of MPs (including some Ministers) employ at least one family member in their offices, at a total cost to the taxpayer of £5.8 million. Just three out of 200 MPs said they had advertised the post occupied by a member of the family.

The practice of employing family members is outlawed in many other countries. It is even banned in the USA, where corruption is as much a part of politics as bread is a part of a sandwich.

In 1967, the US Congress passed anti-nepotism laws stopping the hiring of family members.

But in the UK, MPs hire as many family members as they can fit onto the pay roll.

It doesn't seem to matter much whether they can do the work or, indeed, whether there is any work for them to do.

229

Fiddling expenses seems to be a full time job for some MPs. It is perhaps not surprising that they don't get any time for politics.

The expenses are supposed to be claimed only when they are essential to the business of being an MP but MPs have claimed tax free payments for biscuits, a trouser press, a kitchen sink (and plug), dog food, repairing heating pipes under a tennis court, preparing a helipad, cleaning out a moat, buying over 500 bags of manure, building a floating duck house and purchasing miscellaneous toiletries. One MP claimed £87,000 for gardening expenses. Another claimed more than £4,000 'to cover the basic costs of grass cutting'. Home Secretary Jacqui Smith accidentally claimed for pornographic movies watched by her husband. The Scottish Chancellor of the Exchequer, Alistair Darling, said he was very sorry for claiming expenses for a flat he wasn't living in while at the same time claiming expenses for the flat he was living in. It was, apparently, just another one of those oversights MPs with too many homes seem to make. (I wonder if taxpayers who make mistakes on their tax forms will now be able to get away with simply apologising for their errors?)

Numerous MPs learned the hard way that not all publicity is good publicity. Just as Richard Nixon is remembered only for Watergate so many MPs will be remembered not for whatever good they did but for their fiddled expenses. I suspect that Smith will be remembered for accidentally allowing taxpayers to pay for pornographic movies while Darling will be remembered for being a little confused about where he lived.

An apparently endless stream of ministers have made claims that millions of self-respecting citizens regard as a horrifying abuse of the system. Ministers who had made solemn pronouncements about the evils of tax avoidance were found to have spent a considerable amount of their own time working out tricky little ways to keep their money out of the hands of the taxman.

Afterwards the excuses were invariably the same; either 'everything I did was within the rules' or 'I made a mistake and didn't mean to claim for the dog-grooming/pornographic movies/ moat cleaning/two houses at a time'.

It's difficult to believe that several hundred MPs have all made serious mistakes with their expenses claims. And it is surprising that all of them seem to have made mistakes in their own favour.

'I may have claimed for X,' said one MP self righteously, 'but I didn't claim for Y.'

'The people don't understand how it works,' said another, patronisingly.

'People who complain are jealous,' said a third.

Others complained that their privacy was being invaded and that they were being made depressed by the all the attention their finances were receiving.

Occasionally, scared of losing voters perhaps, MPs offered

to repay some of the money they had falsely claimed as 'an administrative oversight'. (Burglars should not try this. It is not yet always regarded as an acceptable solution to a crime.)

230

One MP, misjudging the public mood and, presumably, hoping to arouse some sympathy, said that she was worried that one of her colleagues might commit suicide.

'Will he or she be able to claim for the funeral expenses if they do?' asked a reader of one national newspaper, confirming that voters were considerably angrier than MPs suspected.

Millions who had taken little or no interest in politics, felt let down and betrayed.

231

The expenses scandal showed just how petty and tawdry party politics had become.

Men and women who had been elected to lead the country had sold their honour, the respect of their fellow citizens and their dignity for a flat screen television set, a terrace full of pot plants and an armful of cushions.

How terribly, terribly sad. How pathetic.

It is now clear to everyone that the House of Commons is packed with second-rate jobsworths, expense account fiddlers. It was salutary to realise that while the country was heading into economic chaos MPs were studiously working out new ways to cheat taxpayers.

The idea that politicians act rationally, and with our interests at heart, has been banished as false and idealistic. But there is a silver lining: the exposure of MPs as corrupt and petty gives us a once in a lifetime – once in several centuries – opportunity to make a real change in our society.

232

It may be difficult to imagine, but there were days when MPs were men of reputation and great renown. Sir Isaac Newton, Sir

Christopher Wren and John Stuart Mill all once sat in the House of Commons as members of Parliament.

Few, if any, of today's MPs have achieved anything outside winning the support of a parliamentary party. Few of them could. Their only noticeable talents are obsequiousness, the ability to lie (without shame or embarrassment) and the ability to defend themselves without care or thought for their responsibilities, or for the dignity of their position.

233

Maybe MPs think nothing of stealing from taxpayers because it is what governments do. Maybe MPs have simply been corrupted by the system in which they operate.

234

The Global Corruption Barometer survey conducted by Transparency International (a not-for-profit organisation) showed that, when asked to rate people for corruption, the British responded by putting politicians right at the top of the list – above all other groups (but only slightly above the British legislature, whose representatives are also widely regarded as corrupt).

235

When the extent of their abuse of their expenses became public the first response at Westminster was to call in the police – not to arrest thieving MPs and Ministers but to find out how the information had been leaked.

This reminded me of how the Government responded in the 1980s when I published information showing that although the NHS bought supplies by the ton it paid more for toilet rolls, envelopes and soap powder than if it had bought them from a local branch of Tesco.

The official response was to launch an enquiry, not into the waste of money, but into how I'd found out about it.

236

Here are some simple rules which would give us better MPs.

1. It should not be possible for anyone to become an MP under the age of 40.

2. All prospective MPs should have had a real job (i.e. one in the outside world; a job which has nothing to do with politics) for at least 20 years.

3. Politicians should be paid only an honorarium to cover their direct, personal expenses. We need MPs who have enough money not to be seduced by wealth or the chance of fiddling their expenses.

237

We need to deal more harshly with crooked public officials (including civil servants as well as politicians). At the moment, hardly anyone in public life ever resigns. Most cling to their jobs, whatever their failures might be and whatever dishonesties might have been exposed.

The political survival of the oleaginous Peter Mandelson is testimony to our absurd tolerance of inadequate standards in public life. A normal person in his circumstances might possibly have been rewarded with an invitation to accept a stay at one of Her Majesty's less luxurious establishments. Mandelson, however, was rewarded with a job as a European Union Commissioner, together with a huge salary, loads of lovely expenses and a massive pension.

Politicians who misbehave should be fired. They should not receive fat pay offs or great pensions. We can no longer wait for politicians who steal or fiddle or lie to resign.

How do we decide whether or not politicians are guilty of unacceptable behaviour? Simple. We are their employers and so we should decide. Politicians accused of unacceptable behaviour should be tried before a jury – not a judge or some Government appointed one man quango.

238

No Minister or MP should attend private, secret meetings. There's a lot of this going on these days but I am thinking, in particular, of the Bilderberg Group.

It was allegedly at Bilderberg Group meetings that the Treaty of Rome (which created the Common Market) was born. And both Iraq wars were probably born at Bilderberg meetings too.

Those who attend always claim that nothing secretive or conspiratorial goes on. These are, they say, simply private meetings where Prime Ministers, Presidents and bankers can get together. Most of our Prime Ministers for the last forty years have attended. It's the sort of meeting Peter Mandelson goes to.

If Bilderberg meetings are private why do we pay for them? And why is there so much security (which we pay for) and so much secrecy?

Those who attend Bilderberg meetings claim that these private meetings are nothing for the rest of us to bother with or be concerned about.

If world leaders (whose salaries are paid by us) hold meetings with global bankers and we pay the hotel bills, the food bills, the booze bills, the transport bills and the security bills then we are entitled to know what is discussed and what is decided.

And if they refuse to tell us what we've bought with our money then we are entitled to believe that something dodgy and conspiratorial is going on behind closed doors.

239

Members of Parliament should pass some sort of examination to show that they have an IQ of at least 100. I can give a thousand examples illustrating the need for this.

240

Politicians who commit treason should be sent to the Tower of London and exhibited there for life, so that small children can look at them and learn what happens to dishonest politicians.

Edward Heath, the biggest traitor England has ever seen, should be dug up and his undoubtedly still fat skeleton displayed there permanently.

241

All votes should be cast through the ballot box. The political parties introduced postal voting because it gave them a chance to fiddle the results. (It's much easier to fiddle the results when you don't have hordes of people insisting on pushing their ballot paper into a box.)

The political parties are also keen to introduce computerised voting machines (even though the evidence shows clearly that these are easy to rig and are a boon for dishonest politicians). Machines must never be allowed replace the ballot, the ballot box and a band of unpaid, independent scrutineers.

242

There should be no public funding of political parties or parliamentary candidates.

If we ever give money to political parties there will be no hope at all for what remains of our tattered parliamentary democracy.

243

English political parties and politicians are interchangeable. (Actually, to be accurate, most of the politicians aren't English.)

Think of any leading politician. Now imagine him transplanted into another political party. It isn't difficult is it?

There is nothing much to help us distinguish between the three main parties; they have much the same policies and the same arrogance; they display the same indifference to the voters and they make the same mistakes; they share the same taste for power (for its own sake rather than for what it can be used to achieve) and the same denial of reality. All support the power of the State rather than the integrity and freedom of the individual.

The party system is now irredeemably corrupt. The system has been honed by several generations of politicians to reward the corrupt and to punish the incorruptible. I believe it is inconceivable that the system can, or will, produce an honest leader.

Governments act not in the interests of the country but in the interests of the controlling party. So, for example, if a government looks like losing a forthcoming election it will take reckless risks with the economy. If it loses the election some other party will be left to clear up the fiscal mess. If they win they will have another few years of power and money making opportunities.

(Because of the political party system modern politicians are like the bankers who caused the credit crunch crisis. They are encouraged to take risks because they gain if they win but someone else pays if they lose.)

The aims of political parties and individual electors are diametrically opposed. All political parties want more government (because that will give them more power) when what the people want and need is less government (and more freedom).

244

When party politicians talk about change they confine themselves to tinkering. They don't want the system to change very much at all because it suits them very nicely the way things are.

The party politicians, and the media, concentrate their attention on trivialities. Political debates are phoney because they deal with minutiae.

This attitude (concentrate on minutiae and ignore the big issues) has pervaded all areas of public life.

Speaking at the House of Commons some years ago, I provided evidence showing conclusively that animal experiments are so misleading that not even drug companies (their main official advocates) take them seriously.

In the audience, which comprised of interested members of the public as well as MPs, there was a member of an organisation which exists to oppose vivisection.

When I had finished my presentation the anti-vivisectionist stood up and immediately started to talk about the wonderful work his organisation was doing in improving the size of the cages used to transport animals being flown to Britain for use in experiments.

He ignored the facts I had given and the MPs, delighted by the opportunity to avoid embarrassing reality, welcomed his relatively trivial revelations.

And thus it is in all areas of public life these days. The big issues are ignored and suppressed and those who raise them are dismissed as lunatics, heretics or fanatics. Anyone who dares to spread the truth, or raise questions about perceived truths, will be subjected to smear campaigns. Our liberty and our freedom of speech have been strangled by cross party consensus and an obedient media. Politicians and commentators concentrate their efforts on narrow, specific questions. The big questions, the important questions, are never asked. And so, not surprisingly, no answers are forthcoming either.

245

'Truth is treason in the empire of lies'.
TEXAN CONGRESSMAN AND FORMER USA PRESIDENTIAL
CANDIDATE RON PAUL

246

Politics today is primarily about politicians rather than voters. The only people who get anything out of elections are the politicians.

247

It is hardly surprising that voting turnouts are forever falling. These days barely half the electorate bother to turn out to use their vote. Why? Simple. People don't vote because the politicians aren't worth voting for. And the party system means that people know that unless they live in a marginal constituency, and the election is likely to be a close one, their vote will be worthless. If political parties were banned and electors were invited to vote for independent candidates the turnout would rocket.

Voters know that elections are a sham. There are no real choices. All our major political parties are fundamentally fascist; they want to tyrannise us and impose their beliefs on us. Instead of wanting to create a free and liberated society, where we can all get on with our lives, they want to expand their control over our lives and they want to interfere in every aspect of everything we do.

All today's political parties want to violate our individual rights and to increase the rights of government. Those views are fundamentally fascist.

The three parties control what happens. And yet the three party system is a confidence trick. MPs who are members of the three parties represent (and vote for the interests of) their parties rather than the electors or the country.

Most people don't vote in European, parliamentary or local government elections because there doesn't seem much point. There isn't any significant difference between the parties. Politicians don't take any notice of what the voters want. And they don't keep their promises. Politicians are so focused on the next election that they never think of the next generation.

248

We must take back the political power which is rightfully ours. We have to take back power from the crooks and the crooked institutions which now rule our lives. We have to take back power from the weak, spineless and unthinking politicians who serve those institutions with such uncritical faithfulness.

The people are now the only force of opposition; the only voice for freedom and justice is the voice on the streets.

England needs a House of Commons made up of independent men and women who will keep their promises, who will stick to their manifestos and who will vote honestly and decently according to their consciences.

Until that happens our destiny, welfare and history will be in the hands of political parties which have their own vested interests to pursue.

249

All organisations (and this is particularly true of political organisations) develop their own (well-hidden) agenda: their own reason for being.

For the first time in history we have succeeded in creating a world, a society, which now exists solely to defend, protect and develop itself.

We have created a society whose institutions have acquired power of their own. These institutions – governments, multinational corporations, multinational bureaucracies and so on – now exist solely to maintain, improve and strengthen themselves.

These institutions have their own hidden agendas and the human beings who work for them may think that they are in control – but they aren't.

Political parties exist to provide comfortable employment for the paid employees, social support groups for voluntary workers (who usually spend most of their time concerned with constitutional minutiae and fighting one another for power within the organisation) and power, money and status for the party's political representatives: the MPs and the councillors.

Political parties exist to win seats and to win elections. That is all they exist for.

The interests of the modern political party no longer match the original aims of the founders; they are far removed from the original concerns and passions which led to their development.

The Labour Party doesn't really care about the English people or about England. The Labour Party doesn't care whether England exists or disappears; it doesn't care about Scotland, Wales or Northern Ireland; it doesn't care about the NHS, the railways or the security of old people in Birmingham, Manchester or Leeds.

The Labour Party is an organisation, and organisations don't have feelings, passions or purposes. Organisations exist only to exist. And, as with so many organisations, the Labour Party is run by salaried employees and voluntary workers whose primary aim must be to sustain and strengthen the organisation.

The same thing is true of the Conservative Party. And the Liberal Democrat Party. And in the end it will be the same of any large, successful political party. These institutions have agendas of their own and those who appear to run them are, in truth, simply institutional servants; their role is to ensure the survival of the institution they serve.

131

(This is also true of companies, charities and all other modern, large institutions. The people who run them may think they are in charge but they aren't; the institution has its own needs (such as good quarterly results in the case of a company) and the directors and managers are there to serve the institution's needs. If they do well then the institution will reward them generously.)

250

Our first step to freedom must be to free ourselves of the 'party system' and return to the days when our Parliament consisted of honest, caring individuals whose only concern was the future safety and welfare of the people they represented – and the country of which they were citizens.

And that will be a real (and bloodless) revolution.

251

It is not the duty of a government to micro-manage people's lives. It is the duty of a government to provide a safe, effective, unobtrusive infrastructure which allows citizens the freedom to do their own thing.

Ayn Rand, the author of *Atlas Shrugged* and the founder of the philosophy of objectivism, declared that the only true purpose of politics is to protect individual rights. And she was right.

252

It will take some time to get rid of the party system. But once there are a few genuinely independent MPs in Parliament the present dishonest system will start to crumble. How will the party whips respond when a growing number of MPs cannot be bullied or bribed into acting in a particular way?

As the number of independent MPs grows so the power of the parties will collapse. Eventually, the independent MPs in the House of Commons will have the majority. They will be able to form a Government themselves. And the parties will be finished. We will have a House of Commons populated by rational, individual MPs who are not driven by absurdities such as political correctness and multiculturalism and who are responsible, as individuals, for representing a relatively small part of the country.

253

If we had a House of Commons consisting entirely of independent members of Parliament we would not have sent troops to Iraq or Afghanistan.

We started two wars because they suited the leaders of the ruling political party. And because the ruling political party could tell individual members of Parliament how to vote. The party system has betrayed us and it's time we changed it. The Government should be the servant of the Commons and the Commons should be the servant of the people. That's not the way it is at the moment.

254

Because of our party system, politicians think no more than four years or so ahead and constantly advocate harmful short-term policies designed to benefit not the nation but their own party interests.

255

At election time individual candidates should announce what they stand for (rather than what they think the public want to hear, or what they are told to say because it is what someone in London has been hired to believe). The voters can then select their candidate, instead of having their choice made for them by a bunch of local party hacks who have chosen a candidate to be promoted.

256

'Those who are unafraid to say they do not know become wise. Those who insist they know never learn. Those who pay attention to their weaknesses gain strength. Wisdom and strength come from the courage to see things as they are.'
TAOIST PHILOSOPHY

257

The House of Commons is a hideous melange of corruption, depravity and vulgarity; an oozing mass of pustulant excrescences. Favouritism is rife. We are ruled by battalions of mediocrities.

The Government interferes in every aspect of our lives, and pokes its nose into every detail of our affairs. Groups of people whom the establishment favours benefit according to prejudices and favouritism.

Millions now rely entirely upon the State for their prosperity. Those who rely upon their own wits and hard labour are at a huge disadvantage. The Government has taken upon itself the right to dispense good and evil according to personal whims. As William Leggett predicted, the State has assumed 'the functions which belong to an overruling Providence'. The public are fleeced and the fortunate benefit.

258

What have we done to deserve MPs who signed us up to the Lisbon Treaty – giving away a thousand years of history and freedom – without even bothering to read the cursed document? Most of our MPs and ministers would be better suited to employment requiring manual rather than intellectual effort (though you'd have to count the tools at the end of the day). Modern party politicians are constantly reaching for mediocrity; stretching every sinew in their bloated bodies as they grapple with simple competence. Always failing. And in politics, as in stagnant ponds, the scum always rises to the top.

Is it really impossible to find a few hundred honest and honourable men and women in England?

259

What sort of world have we created in which a man such as Mandelson can emerge from the shadows of shame to take decisions which affect the very essence of our lives?

(As a trivial aside, it was revealed in spring 2009 that since returning from the EU Mandelson had been spending £500 a week of taxpayers' money on flowers for his office. He had obviously picked up some expensive habits while in Brussels. Not that Mandelson was the only one busy at the florist's. The Labour Government spent a total of £780,000 of taxpayers' money on flowers between 2005 and 2009.)

What sort of world have we created when MPs and peers cheat so much they don't even know when they are doing it? Time and time again politicians and their chums get away with stuff that would result in you or I being locked up for long periods of time.

Lord Ahmed, a Muslim peer who is said to be a leader of the Muslim community and who took his oath on the Koran rather than the bible, was jailed for 12 weeks after texting on a motorway and killing a 28-year-old man. Now, you and I might imagine that 12 weeks was a pretty light sentence. He broke the law. Someone died. But Ahmed, a Justice of the Peace, was released from prison after serving just 16 days. Was I really the only person in the country who found this shocking almost beyond belief? What would the court have done if that had been John Prescott? Sorry, silly choice. Try again. What would the court have done if that had been Vernon Coleman? I can't help thinking that they wouldn't just have thrown away the key but they would have melted it down and turned it into a commemorative medal.

260

Most people believe that most people are telling the truth most of the time. So professional party politicians, who lie most of the time, get away with it.

Modern party politicians lie as effortlessly and as naturally as they breathe. It is an involuntary reflex. Put in modern computer terminology, it is their default position.

261

Politicians are far too cosy and self-regarding. The party system has become conspiratorial rather than confrontational.

Consider what happened after the death of the son of Conservative Party leader David Cameron.

This was a personal tragedy.

But, in an orgy of concern, Parliamentary business was suspended so that 646 MPs could mourn with Mr Cameron. His family loss disrupted the nation's democratic process.

Do you think I am being heartless in criticising this?

OK, look at this another way.

Imagine that a bus driver in London has lost his son. It is just as tragic and as personal a loss as the Cameron loss.

Do all the bus drivers in London stop work to mourn?

Of course they don't.

Imagine that a doctor loses his son.

Do all the doctors in the country stop work so that they can mourn?

Of course they don't.

262

And here's another thing.

Have you noticed that politicians always claim that their families are 'private'. Their children must not be photographed. Questions about whether or not they have been vaccinated are dismissed as intrusive.

And yet, the moment a politician is in trouble, the first thing he does is drag out his wife, his children, his parents, his in-laws and his dog for the cameras. If the children are ailing that's even better.

If party politicians can't win your vote any other way they will do it with sympathy.

'Look at me. You've got to vote for me. My budgie is sick.'

Ruthless and uncaring.

263

The standard modern political solution when faced with having said something or done something stupid, wrong and embarrassing is to do the political two step. They all do it. The first step is to stick by your original story. You defend your actions unreservedly.

The second step is to change your original story. You repeatedly requote yourself saying something slightly different, but to your advantage.

Your critics will become confused and will spend time arguing about precisely what you said rather than what you did.

Crisis averted.

264

Most MPs are merely bit part actors, fit to open fetes, kiss babies and write patronising, self-glorifying rubbish for the local newspaper.

A vote for a back bencher in any party is a wasted vote because he or she will creep to their party leaders and will do nothing to help the local community that might upset the all–important relationship with the party.

A vote for a party leader may give a constituency some dubious infamy but such politicians will rarely have the time or the inclination to bother themselves overmuch with constituents' problems.

265

'In all affairs, it's a healthy thing now and then to hang a question mark on the things you have long taken for granted.'
BERTRAND RUSSELL

266

The vast majority of rebels and dissenters are decent, honest, honourable people who care about their country and what happens to it.

The Government, however, controlled by whichever party happens to be in power, fears dissent and argument because such things threaten its power and its very existence and so, in the false name of suppressing terrorism, it suppresses all dissent; doing everything it can to punish and silence anyone who dares to speak out.

The media, which ought to be on the side of the dissenters

(every journalist worth his salt should be a natural anarchist) has become beholden to the controlling party for two reasons.

First, the controlling party can make commercial life easier or harder for the company behind the publisher or broadcaster, and high level corporate employees prefer 'easier' because it translates readily into 'profitable'.

Second, journalists have been flattered into silence on important issues by being given neatly packaged stories, carefully rehearsed and sanitised scoops, invitations to dinner and gongs in the honours lists. The majority of journalists spend their days rewriting corporate press releases and then either reading them out or printing them. It doesn't much matter if the press release comes from an arms manufacturer or a government department.

If you think I am exaggerating ask yourself one simple question: when did you last read or hear a journalist or commentator criticising the party system of government we now regard as fundamental and inevitable?

And things are set to get worse. The BBC has a pro EU bias and yet soon for many people the BBC may be the only source of news. Commercial television stations talk of their inability to continue with local news programmes.

267

You have three choices: you can put up with the party system and allow anger and resentment to burn holes in your soul; you can go abroad to live; or you can stay and fight and change the system by getting rid of political parties.

268

Time is running out and we must act fast.

Our existing political parties are giving away more and more power to America and to the EU. We must act before the Government has given away everything.

If you want to join the bloodless revolution the requirements are very simple.

Make sure that you always vote for an independent candidate.

Do not, under any circumstances, vote for a candidate representing one of the main three parties.

That's it.

If we do this then we can break the three-in-one party system which has for so long held a stranglehold over British politics and we can fill Parliament with people who care about nothing but the voters and the country.

Our representatives will know that if they fail to represent the wishes of the voters, or at least satisfy the voters that they have voted honestly and honourably, then they won't be elected at the next election. Their political future will be in the hands of the voters, not the party.

Getting rid of political parties will also get rid of the absurdity whereby the country may be governed by a political party which has received a minority of the overall vote. (An absurdity which will not be removed by fiddling with the system and introducing schemes such as proportional representation.)

Joining the bloodless revolution really is that simple: vote not for the party but for the individual. Always vote for an independent candidate. Never vote for a party candidate. Pick the candidate you think will best represent your interests.

269

And tell all your friends why they should avoid voting for a party candidate.

If, between us, we can reach enough people then the bloodless revolution is guaranteed to work.

270

Even if your independent candidate turns out to be an incompetent crook we will all be better off. One incompetent and crooked MP can do far less damage than an incompetent and crooked political party.

271

Independent MPs have an enormous amount of power in the

House of Commons. They can do a great deal of good for their local constituents. The vote of an independent MP cannot be relied upon by a big party machine. An independent MP cannot be told to vote one way or the other. He cannot be threatened with expulsion from the party or bribed with a promise of minor office or a peerage. The independent MP is far better placed to represent the interests of the people who sent him to Parliament. If he doesn't vote with their interests in mind they won't vote for him again. The independent MP can demand things for his constituency and have a reasonable hope that his demands will be met. He will, at the very least, have a much greater hope of success than the MP who represents a party – whether that party be in or out of power.

Voting for independent candidates will give us back our parliament and our country. Our votes will count for the first time in our lives.

At the beginning of each new Parliament, independent MPs must vote and choose from among their number a group of leaders.

272

When, a decade or so ago, I first recommended that we should stop voting for the big three political parties I recommended that electors should, instead, vote for smaller political parties which offered a manifesto with which they felt comfortable.

I now think that this was a serious mistake. (In words never uttered by political leaders: 'I was wrong.')

This sort of voting will merely perpetuate the party system. The problem is that small political parties, like big ones, have an agenda of their own. The small political party wants to become a big political party so that it can acquire power and authority. Its driving members are likely to be motivated by personal ambition rather than a desire to improve the world.

The only long-term solution is to avoid voting for any candidates standing on behalf of any political party – however small that party might be.

The bloodless revolution will come only if we vote only for

truly independent candidates; men and women who are driven by passion and who are so bloody-minded that they would never fit comfortably into any political party.

Voting for individuals rather than parties gives us a chance to change the country in one day.

An instant, polling day, revolution.

We only need to win once and the party system will be finished. The bloodless revolution will be the most peaceful revolution in world history.

273

When we have got rid of the parties there will be many things we can do which we were never be able do while our country was ruled by, and for the benefit of, one or other of the political parties.

Without political parties controlling the country everything will change. Parliament, made up of hundreds of independent MPs, will do what those MPs (and, therefore, their constituents) really want to happen.

Nothing will be impossible.

In the final section of this book I've explained some of the things we *could* do if we had a parliament full of, and controlled by, individual MPs who were responsible not to the requirements of a political party but to the electors who had voted for them.

274

'...for on his choice depends
The safety and the health of the whole State.'
SHAKESPEARE (HAMLET)

275

The parties will, of course, stick together and claim that all this is impossible. They are, of course, lying.

The *Financial Times* claims that independent candidates have no hope of office and could only make an impact by joining with other independent candidates to form a new party.

This is unimaginative nonsense.

A Parliament of independent MPs, and a ban on political parties, will lead to a fairer, more honest, more respectful democracy. It will mean defeat for the fascists who have controlled our lives for too long.

276

Please help spread the word.

Your part in the revolution began when you picked up this book. You now know what has to be done. It is very simple. It is perfectly legal. You can't get into trouble. And it's bloodless.

If you agree with the basic premise of this book (that we need a bloodless revolution) then please lend copies of this book to everyone you know. Share the great adventure with as many people as possible.

Copies of *Bloodless Revolution* are available from Publishing House at very low prices. *Please see the advertisement at the back of this book for details.*

277

Revolutions are only impossible before they take place. Afterwards they were inevitable.

Part Two

Two Dozen Life Changing Things We Can Do (If We Want To) When We've Got Rid Of Political Parties

We all have different goals, needs and rights and we are all entitled to put forward our views. In a properly run democracy, discussions, even about contentious issues, should be conducted openly, with respect and with an understanding that we all have varying aims, beliefs and aspirations.

You may not agree with everything in this book. Indeed, I'd be surprised if you did. That doesn't matter. I hope, however, that you will agree with me that the original, creative proposals in Part Two of this book are at least worth discussing. Without the constraints of a party system (a system with its own needs, quite separate from those of the population) we would be able to manage our lives with imagination and flair. On the pages that follow I've suggested ideas that a Parliament of independent political representatives could consider. Every single one of these proposals is affordable and would change our lives dramatically. Not one of them would be considered – let alone put into practice – by a government run by a political party.

1. We should have regular referenda on big issues.

Every major decision can and should be challenged by a referendum. Party politicians are terrified of them because they put power into the hands of the people. But that, surely, is as good a reason as any to have them. Switzerland, probably the only truly democratic country in the world, holds regular referenda so that its people can vote whenever important issues are being debated. This system works perfectly well there and Switzerland is now widely acknowledged to be the most democratic country in the world.

Political parties do not like referenda and will do everything they can to avoid offering them to the electorate. When the people are allowed to vote on important issues they have a nasty habit of providing conclusions which do not suit political parties.

So, for example, Gordon Brown and the Labour Party refused to allow a promised referendum on the Lisbon Treaty (handing control of England, Scotland, Wales and Northern Ireland to the unelected bureaucrats of the European Union) because he and they knew that the public would vote against it. And so the Lisbon Treaty was signed against the wishes of the majority of the British people.

2. We need to overhaul our voting system.

We need to reconsider the principle of 'one man one vote'. Voting in England has become something of a joke in recent years. Shareholders who vote against company directors' pay are likely to have their vote ignored. Television viewers who pay to vote for selected contestants in reality show competitions may find that their votes have not been counted – even though they have been charged. And electors who vote in parliamentary elections are wasting their time. Political manifestos, controlled by parties which have no interest in the welfare of the electors or the country, are an irrelevance. No one takes them seriously. Politicians know that they will ignore them. And so do the voters.

Politicians know that they can safely ignore the wishes of the electorate as a whole as long as they cater for the whims and wishes of a small, controlling group of voters. This small controlling group consists of those who rely upon the State for their income – either as employees or as dependants.

The people who voted for the Labour Party at the last election did so for purely personal, selfish reasons. They didn't do it because they thought that the Labour Party would make the nation a better, fairer country. They didn't believe that the Labour Party would look after the sick, the frail and the disadvantaged more wisely and more compassionately than any other party. They didn't believe that the Labour Party would provide a better infrastructure, or defend the nation's interests with more vigour, more determination and more loyalty.

They voted for the Labour Party because they believed that in doing so they would best preserve their benefits.

The politicians who run the country are self-serving and the people who put them in power are self-serving too.

The time has come to reconsider the validity and fairness of the sacred principle of 'one man one vote'.

It is generally accepted that the principle of one man (or woman) one vote is a fair and just one, but the truth is that this method of voting has created a society in which those who work, pay tax and (literally) support society are ruled by an unholy alliance of those who either fail to work at all (because they are unemployed, unemployable, sick or lazy) and those who work for the State.

The original concept of giving every man and woman a vote was based on the unarguably fair notion that everyone who contributes to society should have a say in how it is run.

But when the vote was given to all, it was never envisaged that a dominant part of the voting would end up in the hands of the unemployed, the long-term sick, the non taxpayers, the professional users and the parasites; takers not givers.

Things have changed.

Today, it is perfectly possible for a government to win power – and to hold onto it – simply through winning the votes of people who make no contribution to society.

It is because they know that this is where their votes come from that the Labour Party has done nothing to stop the epidemic of benefit fraud which is destroying the Welfare State. The Labour Party doesn't care two hoots that those who are genuinely in need are being pushed aside and abandoned. All the Labour Party cares about is staying in power and enjoying the perks and the money that come with the power. If this means pandering to those who prefer not to work then this is what they will do.

So many millions now receive State benefits, and are wholly dependent upon the Government for their income, that all political parties now pander to them, in order to win their votes, while at the same time ignoring the needs and rights of those who work and pay tax.

Today, a political party can win an election with 20% of the national vote. And a party can reach this vote by pandering to and attracting the votes of the unemployed, those receiving incapacity benefits, public sector workers and scroungers. The Labour Party has, for years, been deliberately enlarging this group in order to protect the party's electoral success. The result is that taxpayers are disenfranchised. The country is run on behalf of people who are 'takers', who contribute nothing but who take a great deal.

Things have gone too far. Today, the inmates are running the asylum for their own benefit.

Votes should now be limited to those who contribute.

It is a long-standing part of our electoral tradition that prisoners do not receive a vote. Why, after all, should people who do not make a positive contribution to society have a say in how society is run? (It is worth noting, however, that the European Union plans to change this and to give votes to prisoners.)

It would make just as much sense to withdraw the right to vote from those who are long-term benefit claimants, or who never work. Voting rights could, perhaps, be given only to those who have worked and paid tax for, say, twenty years. Those rights, once given, would be for life. State employees would not be on the voting register unless they had worked outside the State system for twenty years.

Our present system is ludicrous and quite unfair. It's like allowing those who receive donations from a charity to decide how the charitable contributions should be distributed and how much those who contribute to the charity should give. Why should people who choose to never pay tax have any say at all over how taxes are raised or spent?

In a fair world only private sector taxpayers would be entitled to a vote.

In our current system taxpayers pay for everything, are

constantly persecuted and abused by the authorities and receive very little in return.

No political party would contemplate even discussing the change I have suggested. The big three political parties know that their power depends upon their being able to buy votes from those electors who are dependent upon the Government and who will, therefore, vote for whichever political party offers them the biggest bribes.

3. Central and local governments should relinquish all control over transport.

Governments of all sizes have proved themselves incapable of managing complex transport services efficiently or economically. Allowing central and local governments to have any sort of control over the provision of transport facilities has been disastrous.

Since a previous Government listened to the illogical arguments of Dr Beeching and closed numerous railway lines (and railway stations) the quality of transport in England has deteriorated year by year. Train services are now among the dirtiest and least reliable in the world. Public transport is poor and expensive and as a result roads are overcrowded. Because they are overcrowded roads constantly need extensive, expensive and disruptive repairs.

Whenever they are given the authority to run, or to regulate, transport services politicians create chaos.

Road repairs (constantly required because of the over-use resulting from the closure of much of the nation's railway network) mean that delays on English roads are the norm rather than the exception. It is difficult to drive for an hour in England without being held up at least two or three times by roadworks.

Why aren't roads mended at night? In China, road repairs are done at night so that motorists and lorry drivers are inconvenienced as little as possible – and to reduce the cost to the economy. (In Japan, all repairs to the rail network are done between the hours of midnight and six a.m. The Japanese did try doing track repairs in the daytime once during the 1980s but there was so much protest that they've never done it again.) The small extra costs involved (paying overtime to workmen and putting up lights to illuminate the site) are minute compared to the money saved by allowing people to move around without long delays.

But our councils and governments do not operate for the benefit of the community – they operate for their own convenience and profit.

The answer is simple: all transport should be provided by private companies and roads should be paid for by tolls. If all roads were toll roads then the people who owned and ran them would want to keep them open to keep the traffic moving, in order to maximise profits. They would have an incentive to do repairs at night. (The incentive could easily be formalised with a contract requiring all toll road owners to do repairs outside peak hours.)

A system of tolls would be fairer than car taxes or fuel taxes.

There is absolutely no need for government (local or central) to have any direct involvement in the provision of transport facilities.

4. All small post offices, schools, railway lines and hospitals which have been closed should be reopened.

In a world where oil is going to become increasingly expensive it makes good sense to minimise the amount of travelling people have to do – and to improve public transport by reopening train stations and train lines. The closure of small post offices (under orders from the European Union) means that queues at the remaining post offices cost the country several billion pounds a year in wasted time.

5. We need to get rid of at least 90% of all the red tape governing our lives.

The British Chambers of Commerce estimates that red tape and regulations cost us £77 billion a year. That's £77 billion wasted every year on largely pointless, always intrusive bureaucratic nonsense. And the sum wasted is rocketing by 10%–20% a year. We need to get rid of at least 90% of the red tape. It probably doesn't matter which 90% we get rid of.

Bureaucrats and modern party politicians love regulations for it is regulations (invariably given the full force of the law, even though they are devised without troubling the usual democratic processes) which expand their power and increase their control.

The drive for more regulations is endless. Those wishing to open bank accounts will doubtless soon need to give blood samples and attend a lengthy interview in Sunderland before being considered suitable applicants.

Regulatory bodies invariably attract employees who are self-important, aggressive, inconsistent, intolerant, hubristic, evangelistic, hypocritical, sanctimonious. Ordinary citizens, the people who are supposed to be protected by regulations and regulators, are the people who suffer most from their very existence. Regulatory burdens which restrict and inhibit need to be removed and replaced with incentives. (The carrot works better than the stick).

We will all benefit enormously if we get rid of all regulatory bodies and all government quangos. None of them is worth a light. Regulation is expensive and intrusive and has proved itself entirely useless. Worse, it often encourages a feeling of complacency. Banks, for example, assume that if they satisfy the regulators they are doing everything they need to do. And customers assume that because there are regulators they are protected. Both are wrong. Everyone would be better served if our regulators were disbanded and the billions wasted on their upkeep made available as compensation to those who have been cheated.

The Financial Services Authority (FSA) is probably the most expensive and least worthwhile of all our current quangos. The FSA, a bonanza for bureaucrats, has created a host of pointless, petty rules with which to inconvenience honest people but has ignored the big picture and the serious crooks. The organisation failed miserably to prevent the problems associated with the banks in 2007 and 2008. However, the mass of regulations they introduced made it nigh on impossible for people without passports or driving licences to open bank accounts and made every day life pointlessly difficult for millions. Their regulations, devised by an army of ridiculously overpaid bureaucrats with a woeful misunderstanding of the nation's needs, did nothing useful but enormously increased the danger of identity theft and created endless opportunities for crime. If ever there was a need for clear proof that regulation does not work the Financial Services Authority has provided it. It was no surprise at all to learn that at the end of a period when sensitive human beings might have been wearing sack cloth and ashes, and refusing to accept their monthly pay cheques on the grounds that they had failed miserably to do what they were being paid to do, the employees of the FSA were handing one another massive bonuses - probably the least deserved bonuses in history. (Employees of the FSA can receive bonuses of up to 35% of their annual salary. Many of these employees earn over £100,000 a year.)

If there were no Government regulators, businesses would have to build up a reputation for honesty and integrity. This takes some years. There are huge incentives to building up a reputation for honesty and decent dealing. Regulators, however, simply replace these natural driving forces with fear. Behind every piece of regulation issued by a Government regulated quango is a prison cell or a gun. That's how governments always enforce their laws and regulations. Threats replace the natural incentive of developing a decent reputation.

Regulations are bad for everyone for many reasons.

First, all a regulated business has to do is to please the regulators. It doesn't need to develop a decent reputation. All it needs is a bit of paper showing that it knows how to jump through the right hoops with the requisite enthusiasm. Regulatory systems reward the creeps and punish the imaginative and the hard-working.

Second, a government regulated system suggests that all companies (however long-established) are the same; are all crooked and must all be controlled. The implication is that all companies with the proper 'certificate' on the wall are equal. This is clearly nonsense.

Third, official government standards are regarded as minimum standards. And so that's all that customers get. No company can afford to offer a better service because there is no value to integrity. All companies have to do is obey the regulators who have replaced the customers as the arbiters of success and satisfaction. Builders, for example, cannot offer more than the basic building code observance because to do so will cost them money and push up their prices. Quality goes down to the lowest common denominator.

Fourth, government regulators exist to prevent things happening. The bureaucrats get no prizes (or bonuses) if something good comes through the system but they might get their knuckles rapped (though not lose their bonuses) if something bad happens. So they become increasingly officious and repressive. New ideas and improvements tend to be squashed. The regulatory system acts against genuine improvement because no one cannot introduce anything innovative which doesn't fit into the existing rules. This guarantees stagnation.

Fifth, when things go wrong the regulators are concerned solely with protecting themselves and making sure that they get no blame.

Sixth, the enormous costs of regulation mean that the quality of services and goods has to be dragged down. It is because money is spent on satisfying the regulators that when you ring your bank you speak to someone on another continent.

Seventh, excessive regulation destroys the quality of life by making day to day transactions far more complicated than they need to be.

Eighth, the regulatory system has made life easier for the dishonest people. Their crookery is easier to hide and more difficult to find. Sophisticated crooks use the system to steal from everyone (including taxpayers). The only people who have benefited from the regulatory system are the regulators themselves; the highly paid armies of bureaucrats.

Ninth, who regulates the regulators? Who will judge the judges? The system assumes that the regulators are intrinsically more honest than business people. This is patently not true.

Tenth, many of the regulations which exist today have been created at the request of large international businesses which encourage the introduction of new rules because they know that these make it difficult for small competitors to grow. Special interest lobbyists, acting on behalf of pressure groups, help introduce many of the most senseless regulations. Any benefits these regulations might bring are far outweighed by the costs. But since the costs are borne only by the people who are suffering from the regulations the instigators and the advocates of the rules lose nothing.

Ron Paul, USA congressman and former Presidential candidate, tells a revealing story in his book *The Revolution*. He describes how when Senator George McGovern retired from public life he became the proprietor of a small hotel. After two and a half years the hotel was forced to close and Senator McGovern was honest enough to question the regulations which he himself had helped to implement. 'Legislators and government regulators must more carefully consider the economic and management burdens we have been imposing on US business,' he said.

McGovern described how fire regulations meant that he was told that his two storey building had to install a costly automatic sprinkler system and new exit doors, even though every guest room had large sliding doors which opened out onto concrete patios. And he added that his manager was forced to spend days at a time on needlessly complicated tax forms.

Anyone who has tried to run a business in modern England will share those feelings.

The statists distrust freedom and the free market. They have replaced the idea of businessmen being rewarded for their honesty by a system in which the only incentives are fear and force. Small-minded Gestapo-style bureaucrats, given the power to snoop on everyone, have replaced morality and inventiveness. The regulatory system offers a perverse incentive to people to behave badly and to find ways to get round the rules.

It was the regulators who allowed bankers to take huge risks with our money. If the bankers won their bets, they got to keep the profits. If they lost we lost money. And all was fine and dandy as long as the banks obtained copies of passports and driving licences from would-be customers in order to keep the regulators happy. Not only did the regulators not prevent the credit crunch, they actually contributed to it.

The bottom line is that we need far fewer regulations. We are encouraged to believe that rules and regulations are essential and always 'a good thing'. Anyone who suggests that we should have fewer regulations is regarded as a reckless idiot who would be willing to sacrifice safety and good health and fairness for economy, simplicity and freedom. We are encouraged to believe that every new law that is introduced (whether originating in Brussels or London) is vital.

But if we repeal all the regulations that exist, and stick with a few simple basic laws requiring people to behave decently and honourably to one another, we would be far, better off.

Leaving the European Union will instantly rid us of most of the regulations which now stifle entrepreneurs.

6. The police should not be run by local or central government.

Trust between the police and the public has broken down completely. Too many innocent, law-abiding citizens now regard the police as a greater threat to their safety than the villains against whom the police are paid to provide protection.

A major factor in the breakdown of trust has been the increasing politicisation of the police; the use of the police as a revenue gathering entity, and the use of the police to suppress entirely lawful dissent that the authorities find embarrassing or inconvenient.

The function of a police force is very simple: it is the job of the police to patrol our streets and to protect the safety and security of citizens and their property.

In order to do this efficiently, economically and fairly it is now clear that we need a police force which is neither paid for nor regulated in any way by central government but which is recruited and paid locally. The Home Office has repeatedly proved itself incapable of managing anything more complicated than a children's party.

Our police forces should be hired and managed locally for the protection of the community. Local communities can provide better, fairer, more effective police forces at much lower cost. (There should, nevertheless, be a small, well-trained, national team of police officers who can be called in by local forces to deal with particularly challenging crimes. Something along the lines of the old-fashioned Scotland Yard would serve perfectly satisfactorily.)

The current police force is lazy and wasteful and chooses its priorities according to the requirements of politicians (speed cameras producing money from easy to target motorists) rather than the requirements of the public (safe streets and low crime rates).

Crime rates everywhere in England are soaring. Everyone with functioning brain tissue agrees that nothing prevents crime more effectively than putting policemen on the beat. Even senior policemen admit that this is true. So, why doesn't it happen? First, thanks to the Labour Government, the police now spend most of their time filling in forms. Second, the police are too busy doing stuff that will earn money (such as sitting on motorway bridges with speed cameras) to worry about tackling crime.

The police spend millions studying ways to improve the service they offer. They don't need to spend a penny. The village idiot could tell them the answer: put more bobbies on the beat.

Only by putting control back into the hands of local communities (and distancing policing from party politicians) will this happen.

7. Planning should be entirely left to local communities.

The four worst things about town planning offices are the unpredictability and inconsistency of their decisions, the costs, the delays and the corruption.

Applicants, whether they are individuals wanting to build a modest extension or builders wanting to build a housing estate, are entitled to a speedy reply (whether it is yes or no) and a simple appeals process. Central Government should not have any role in planning issues. All decisions are better made when they are taken as close as possible to the area concerned.

8. Immigration needs to be controlled.

Visiting London these days is like visiting a city in a foreign country. When my wife and I visited the city recently we did not hear an English voice, other than that of a cab driver, for two hours after arriving in the capital. Every shop assistant, every waiter and every waitress spoke at best only broken English. The English will soon be able to claim that they are a minority group in what was once their own country.

The people of England know that their history, their culture, their present and their future have been badly damaged by badly managed immigration policies. And it is England that suffers most. A staggering 92% of immigrants stay in England, with the result that although England's population is only five times larger than that of Scotland, Wales and Northern Ireland, England takes in 11 times as many immigrants as the other three parts of the United Kingdom put together.

'You cannot simultaneously have free immigration and a Welfare State,' said Milton Friedman, the economist. What you do get, when you have a Welfare State and free immigration, is a huge budget deficit and growing resentment. And when you have free immigration and a National Health Service which is free to all users you end up with a health care system which is doomed to fail.

It is no wonder that the infrastructure in England (which receives less money than that elsewhere in the UK) has crumbled.

Countless thousands of students come to England every year. Around 10,000 come from Pakistan alone. Every year. Why? We have plenty of our own students. And we don't educate *them* properly. Our children are leaving school unable to read or write properly and we're importing students? (Many of whom, thanks to the Labour Party's wars hate us and want to blow us up.)

Current policies are creating massive resentment (and future race problems). English families should always take preference over asylum seekers and immigrants when housing is being provided. I have been a taxpayer for over 40 years but cannot claim benefits because I have always been self-employed. However, Poles and Romanians and other EU immigrants can claim a full range of benefits without ever having worked here or paid taxes.

If you are white and were born in England then in some parts of your native country you are now (officially) a member of an ethnic minority. (For that reason, if for no other, it should now be clear that immigration needs to be controlled.)

An independent parliament, free of party control, would quickly introduce new immigration policies which would dramatically limit the number of foreigners moving to live in England.

It is an uncomfortable but nevertheless inescapable and undeniable fact of life that some cultures regard tolerance as a sign of weakness. 'We all laugh at the English,' said one Polish immigrant. 'You are all so weak. We come here because you give us money. That is all.'

Bullied and blackmailed by those who preach political correctness and multiculturalism, the English have been far too tolerant.

It's time we stood up for ourselves a little more.

9. We want our privacy back.

The Government should stay out of our personal affairs. Governments should respect our privacy instead of pointing cameras at us wherever we go, listening to our private telephone conversations and reading our private e-mails. (CCTV cameras have been proven to do nothing to prevent crime. But they do provide the State with enormous power. Citizens would be much better off if the money spent on cameras – and people to watch the screens – was spent on more policemen patrolling the streets.)

The idea that politicians should spy on innocent citizens as a right is indefensible in any free nation. That the Government should do these things and pretend that they are protecting us from terrorists and money launderers is absurd. The Government must stop spying on us. This intrusive and rude behaviour doesn't stop terrorism, money laundering or tax evasion.

The Government should also abandon all its computer databases. Government departments and local councils have proved that they cannot be trusted with confidential information; they will either lose it or sell it.

10. We need to re-evaluate our foreign policies.

Our current relations with foreign countries sometimes seem to fall into two categories: there are the countries we are bombing to bits and the countries where we give fairly huge amounts of money to tyrants and dictators who then funnel the money into offshore bank accounts. (The two categories are not always mutually exclusive.)

Our foreign aid policy currently fits into the category of 'poor people in a poor country giving money to rich people in poor countries'. So, every year we give £40 million in aid to China and hundreds of millions to India. These are the richest, most successful new nations on the planet; the world's fastest growing economies. And we are giving them money! If money is changing hands it should be travelling in the other direction.

We need to stop all this nonsense.

Firstly, we can't afford it. Cutting back on the wars started by Blair and approved and continued by Brown will save us billions.

Second, it doesn't do any good. It is time to recognise that our foreign aid policies have done far more harm than good. Vast amounts of money has been spent. Much of it has been used to facilitate dictatorships and genocide. The rest has ended up in secret offshore bank accounts. Even where money has filtered through to poor people it has invariably merely acted as a short-term aid and has done nothing to encourage self-sufficiency. (In the same way that welfare benefits in Britain have ensured that the poor do nothing to become independent.)

Britain, the EU and America could have done far more to help poor countries if they had ensured that surplus food had not been dumped, thereby ruining the chances of indigenous farmers of developing their businesses. The European Union's Common Agricultural Policy is the main cause of starvation in Africa and is directly responsible for millions of deaths and vast amounts of sickness and starvation.

And we should stop selling arms to foreign countries too.

Politicians argue that selling arms helps keep jobs and make money for the nation's companies. But are we really so desperate that we will do anything for money? We could undoubtedly make lots of money by selling off all blonde haired women to Middle Eastern citizens. We could undoubtedly make lots of money by bringing back slavery.

I would rather live in a moderately wealthy country that had morals than in a rich country that had no morals.

I do not suggest for a minute that we declare war on every country whose moral standards are low – we would soon find ourselves at war with a good part of the globe if we did. But we should not allow commerce and profit to interfere with our national moral standards any more than we allow commerce and profit to interfere with our personal moral standards.

I would not personally sell arms for money or gain (or, indeed, for any other reason). I do not buy shares in arms companies. So why should I live in a country which sells arms for gain? It is fair enough that we should manufacture arms to protect ourselves. But, since it is impossible to make judgements about whether other governments will use arms well or cruelly, we should not sell arms to other countries.

England should hold (and uphold) moral principles above commercial gain.

11. *We should abandon the extradition treaties politicians have signed with the USA and the EU.*

The Labour Party gave the Americans the unilateral right to extradite Englishmen and women without providing any evidence that a crime had been committed (or, indeed, having any such evidence). Various Prime Ministers have given the same right to the European Union.

These arrangements should be cancelled. No English citizen should be extradited without having first had an opportunity to hear the evidence against him or her in an English court.

12. *No more money should be spent on translation services.*

England is an English speaking country. Providing translators costs taxpayers hundreds of millions of pounds a year. In future, foreigners who live in England but who do not speak English and who require help must find their own translator (through their own embassy or consulate), just as English citizens must do when living or travelling abroad.

People who choose to live in England should speak the native language – just as we are expected to do in other countries.

An employee in a post office left his job after he apparently embarrassed his employers by saying that he didn't want to serve customers who lived in England but couldn't be bothered to learn to speak English.

Embarrassed?

His employers should have given him a bonus.

13. *Neither governments nor companies should provide pensions.*

We need to change our attitude towards pensions.

Pensions in England fall into two main categories.

First, there are the generous, index-linked pensions paid to former Government and council employees. These pensions are paid by taxpayers and council taxpayers.

Second, there are the far less generous pensions paid to private sector employees. These are paid out of contributions made by employees and employers, and have been made distinctly unattractive by specific legislation brought in by Gordon Brown. Private sector pensions are expensive, highly regulated (usually to the detriment of the pension holders) and often woefully inadequate as a result of high charges and incompetent management. There is also the risk that private sector pensions may at some point be confiscated by a cash hungry Government in search of funds with which to pay public sector pensioners.

There is trouble ahead.

Public sector pensions are a ticking time bomb. They are, quite simply, unaffordable. At what point are we going to abandon them? When the basic rate of income tax reaches 80% and every penny raised is used to provide pensions for former public sector employees? Or are we going to wait until it reaches 100% before we realise that the system is unsustainable?

I've been warning about this problem for two decades and the crisis is now approaching very fast. We do not have, and never will have, the resources to pay public sector pensions to the people who think they are going to get them. Civil servants under 50, who think that when they retire they are going to be guaranteed a fat, index-linked pension are in for a huge disappointment.

Now, here's a question no one ever asks: why should companies, or the State, provide pensions for employees? Why shouldn't people who want a pension be expected to organise (and pay for) their own?

Interesting question.

But here's a better one.

Why do we have pensions at all?

The whole pension industry should die. Without pensions there will be no pensions industry and vast numbers of grasping, greedy bankers, investment advisers and so on will be out of business. The nation will benefit enormously.

How will people survive when they stop working if they have no pensions? There's a simple answer which I will go into further on in this book. I will explain exactly why pensions will be quite unnecessary.

(As an aside, why do the elderly have to retire if they are healthy, willing and able to carry on working?)

None of this will ever change as long as a political party controls our Parliament. Only an independent Parliament would find the courage to make the changes which must be made.

14. We don't torture our prisoners.

In future we do not torture our prisoners, or cooperate with other countries which torture their prisoners. And that includes America.

15. We can, and should, dramatically reduce the number of public sector workers.

There are, currently, around six million public sector workers on the public payroll. (One in fourteen of these is a foreigner.)

That's at least five million civil servants too many. Civil servants work short hours for high pay and have become extremely greedy. During the darkest days of 2009, when most private sector workers were on reduced wages, or in fear of losing their jobs, bin men and some public transport workers were threatening to strike because they were dissatisfied with the pay rises they had been offered.

No government controlled by a political party would dare take this important step.

16. We should get rid of income tax.

England's tax code is by far the most complex and confusing in the world. And our tax rates are now among the highest in the world too. Party politicians will make no fundamental changes to this state of affairs because to do so would be to reduce the extent of their power over the nation's citizens.

There is one simple thing we could do that would revolutionise life for everyone: abolish income tax.

Getting rid of income tax may sound absurd. But it isn't. It is entirely practical. And perfectly possible.

In 2008, the Adam Smith Institute, drawing attention to the consequences of Gordon Brown's decade long reckless spending spree, pointed out that if public spending had only grown in line with inflation since 1997, we could have abolished income tax, corporation tax, capital-gains tax and inheritance tax. And the taxpayer would have been £200 billion better off.

Is there anyone in England who honestly believes that public services were better in 2008 than they were in 1997? If there is then they are deluded for the evidence clearly shows that all this expenditure has resulted in a deterioration, not an improvement, in public services. More children are leaving school unable to read. The NHS is in a far worse condition than it was in 1997. There is more crime. Our roads are in a terrible state. And so on and on. Our infrastructure is crumbling and public services are a disgrace. The money the Labour party spent was wasted on introducing miles of red tape and hiring armies of pointless, bonus-grabbing bureaucrats.

If we abolished income tax, the saving to the nation would be phenomenal. There would be no more time wasted on keeping infernally complex accounts to satisfy the absurd inquisitors working for Her Majesty's Revenue and Customs (HRMC). And Englishmen and women who had left to live in tax exile might well be tempted home again.

Direct taxes – taken out of income – are a massive disincentive. Why bother to work harder if you know that your extra pay is going to be taxed heavily – and that between 25% and 50% of your earnings are going to be commandeered by the government?

The present system is grotesquely unfair. HMRC seems to put little effort into chasing those who pay no tax; it is easier to concentrate on the honest citizens who do pay tax. Like the police (who prefer to harass honest motorists rather than catch dangerous criminals who might well be carrying knives) HMRC prefers to take the easy route. The latest figures show that HMRC detects less than 1.5% of those in the hidden economy. In 2006/7 (the latest year for which figures seem to be available – the civil servants who deal with this stuff are possibly too busy counting their bonuses to produce up-to-date figures, there were just 67 prosecutions out of an estimated two million evaders. These figures were made available to the House of Commons Public Accounts Committee in a report entitled 'HMRC: Tackling the hidden economy'. The report should, perhaps, have had a 'not' in the title somewhere. The figures have not improved since a great many recommendations were made in the Grabiner Report back in 2000.

Getting rid of income tax completely will, of course, solve this problem permanently, and it will allow the hordes currently working for HMRC to find gainful and productive employment which adds value to the nation and to their local communities.

We should also abolish tax on investment income. This would encourage savings and thrift. Why should people be punished for saving money that they have earned?

Spending may well be the oil that keeps society moving, but saving is the foundation upon which financial security is built. Why bother to save money if the government is going to take a cut of whatever interest you receive? (Naturally, the really rich rarely pay income tax at all. They hire lawyers and accountants to ensure that they pay little or nothing in tax on their earnings or profits.)

Instead of taxing hard work and prudence we should tax

only consumption so that people only pay taxes when they spend money. This would encourage savings and discourage inflation. There should be three tax bands. Essentials such as food, heating and books would be zero rated. Non-essentials should be taxed at a medium rate. And luxuries should be highly taxed.

When I first started to write this book I began by thinking that without income tax it would be necessary to raise indirect taxes to quite high levels. It wouldn't. Government spending has grown so rapidly, and to such absurd levels, that indirect taxes do not need to rise at all.

Finally, when councils raise money they should do so through a local poll tax. The last attempt to introduce a poll tax was booted out by demonstrating scroungers who didn't like the idea of having to contribute to the cost of their community. The fact is, however, that a poll tax is the fairest way to raise money and should be used instead of local property taxes. The present system is invidious. Why should people be punished for improving their homes?

Without taxes on capital or labour, and with modest taxes on consumption, investment and productivity will soar and the nation will be increasingly prosperous.

17. We should introduce personal accountability for public employees.

The phrase 'moral hazard' describes the incentive to behave badly because you are insulated from the consequences of your actions. It happens everywhere in the public sector.

Public sector employees have for years taken decisions in the comfortable knowledge that they will not suffer if they make mistakes. That's one of the reasons for the credit crunch.

If a doctor, a lawyer or an architect makes a serious mistake, and is sued, then he must take personal responsibility. Most professionals have insurance to cover themselves for such eventualities.

But when civil servants make serious mistakes they are immune to civil or criminal prosecution. Civil servants are virtually never punished for their misdeeds. If a policeman does something wrong, and is sued, it is the taxpayers who pay whatever damages and costs are awarded against him. If a BBC employee makes a serious mistake, it is licence fee payers (or taxpayers) who are left with the bill. This is patently unfair. And it is particularly nonsensical in that today a great many civil servants receive the carrot of large bonuses (in an attempt to emulate the attractions of private sector employment). It is simply unfair that civil servants should enjoy the carrot but avoid the stick.

All public sector workers should be personally accountable (and legally liable) in exactly the way that doctors and other professionals are liable.

If a doctor screws up (under far more pressure than any public servant) she will get into serious trouble. Why are hospital executives, policemen and others personally immune? Why should the taxpayer pay the fine?

In future all public employees should be personally responsible for any fines, damages and costs they incur through carelessness, bloody-mindedness, wickedness or plain, old-fashioned common or garden stupidity. So, if a policeman is sued for damages, and loses, then he and he alone should be responsible for the bill. If he wants to limit his personal liability then he (like a doctor) should pay for personal liability insurance. It is absurd that taxpayers should pay the bill for crimes committed by public servants.

The Chinese have an effective way of dealing with corrupt or incompetent public officials. They execute them. (If similar standards were upheld in England, the commonest sounds in London would be that of guillotine blades falling and severed heads dropping into baskets.) I have been opposed to capital punishment all my life and consider this a rather over-zealous approach, but we should consider moving a few yards in this direction.

Similarly, when large companies are fined because executives or directors have done something wrong it is invariably the company, and therefore the shareholders, who pay, and the Government (through the fining agency) which benefits. The culprits pay nothing while the truly innocent, the shareholders, are the ones who suffer. This is absurd. Directors and executives receive bonuses when things go well; they should suffer the pain when their incompetence or dishonesty leads to expensive problems. It should be managers and not shareholders who pay when a company is fined for breaking the law.

18. We need to go back onto the gold standard

According to the retail price index, the Great British pound sterling has lost about 95% of its purchasing power since 1956. This means that if you had put a pound under the bed in 1956 you can now buy 5% of what you could buy in 1956.

'Paper money eventually returns to its intrinsic value – zero,' wrote Voltaire, and he was clearly right. Currencies which aren't linked to something tangible (such as gold) aren't worth the paper on which they're printed.

The reason for this fall in the value of our currency is inflation. Politicians usually try to pretend that inflation is caused by prices going up. This isn't true. Inflation is a result of the amount of available money going up. When the Government prints more money the value of the existing stuff goes down. In that respect money is like everything else – the more there is of it the lower the value.

During inflationary periods, the price of petrol, bread or shoes go up because the value of the currency has gone down. And the value of our currency has gone down because the Government has been printing so much of the stuff.

Why have successive Governments printed so much money? Well, the simple answer is that politicians love inflation. They pretend to hate it but really they love it. And they love it because it helps eradicate debt. Getting rid of debt is popular with people who have borrowed loads of money – such as house buyers – but it is particularly popular with the Government which has borrowed more than anyone else.

If you owe £1,000,000 and the value of money falls by half then the amount you owe will also fall by half. (Conversely, Governments everywhere hate deflation because it increases the value of money and therefore increases debts.)

The people who suffer most from inflation are prudent, careful folk who work hard, save some of their money and rarely go into debt. Their savings are destroyed by inflation. The world would be a better and fairer place if we (and other countries around the world) went back onto the gold standard – in other words, if governments were only allowed to issue money for which they had gold or silver backing.

The gold standard was the basis of world finance in the 19th Century but began breaking down during the First World War as governments (specifically Britain) spent huge amounts of money and needed to print more currency than they could back with gold. In the 1930's Britain, the British Empire, France and the USA all abandoned the fixed relationship between their currencies and gold. The gold standard was revived when the dollar became the world's reserve currency, and then American inflation (inflamed by the Vietnam war and American spending) forced President Nixon to abandon the relationship between the dollar and gold in 1971. Since then the world's fiat currencies (printed paper currencies) have lacked any solid basis. The explosion of debt and spending, and the financial excesses of the late 20th Century and early 21st Century, would have been impossible if currencies had all been disciplined by a link to gold.

Going back onto the gold standard would get rid of inflation and eradicate many of the world's most pressing economic problems.

The supply of gold is pretty well fixed; it grows only very slowly and so if we went back onto the gold standard, the value of our money would remain stable. Those who saved would not see their wealth disappear as Governments deliberately printed more money to create inflation.

Why don't governments see the sense in this?

Governments don't like gold because it puts power into the hands of ordinary people who can hold onto it and maintain their wealth despite the Government. And they don't like fixing the currency to a gold standard because it stops them deliberately creating inflation. Indeed, fixing a currency to the gold standard usually creates deflation because as productivity increases so things become cheaper and as things become cheaper so the value of gold rises. Governments hate the idea of that; it means that the debts they acquire by printing more money, in order to acquire more power and to pay for more bureaucrats, will grow instead of shrinking (as they do during inflation).

In March 2009, Russia became the first major country to call for a partial restoration of the gold standard in order to bring some discipline and order back into the world financial system. The Kremlin's chief economic advisor stated that Russia favoured the inclusion of gold bullion in the basket-weighting of a new, manufactured currency to replace the dollar as the world's prime currency. The Chinese realise that a gold-backed currency is vital for financial stability. The Chinese Government is buying tons of gold.

The truth is that gold is a hedge against bad government. And that's the one thing we aren't short of.

A gold based currency would be in the interests of all citizens of England (and, indeed, of all other countries). But no political party would dare introduce a gold-based currency.

19. Schools and colleges should be controlled locally.

If local communities were free to create and run their own schools and colleges, skills, such as literacy and numeracy, would increase and costs would shrink dramatically.

Too many administrators and too many regulations have made education unnecessarily complicated, and have replaced passion with bureaucracy. Today, teaching is less effective at combating illiteracy and innumeracy than it was a century and a half ago.

We do not need a Department of Education. Local communities are perfectly capable of organising and running their own schools without bureaucrats in London telling them what to do. Whenever evidence is published showing that school children are leaving school without being able to read or write the Government responds by hiring more administrators and giving the Department of Education more money. All of this makes things worse.

We need smaller classes and that means that schools need more teachers. And schools need more books. (Forget the computers). As long as schools teach children the basic subjects there won't be any need for a national curriculum.

Thanks to modern educational methods, there are 800 primary schools in England where the majority of 11-year-olds can neither read nor write properly. It's hardly surprising. Under the State's official guidance education has been adapted to ensure that the maximum number of children pass their examinations. In an attempt to hide the fact that British children are now way behind their contemporaries in other countries, examination taking has been turned into a lottery everyone wins. The result is that taking exams these days is like pulling cheap crackers: everyone gets a worthless prize. Pass rates are improved without a commensurate improvement in skills or employability. The State benefits by being able to compare itself favourably with other states. The political party that has been in charge can pat itself on the back at election time. It was the State, and the political parties, which decided that competition was unhealthy and that everyone should have a prize.

It was the State which decided, in order to appease the politically-correct manipulators, that children with special needs should be educated alongside other children and that special schools should, therefore, be closed down. Children of average or above average skills lost out because they were held back while teachers concentrated on the children with special needs. And the children with special needs lost out because they weren't getting the attention they really needed. The State won because it saved money. And the politically-correct won a small and pointless battle in the continuing war on common sense and decency.

It was the State that decided that real skills should be abandoned and that nebulous subjects such as hairdressing and media studies should be given equal weighting to reading and writing. It was through the auspices of the State that pseudo-academic verbiage was created.

We would all save money - and children would be better educated - if local schools were run by local communities. Local people, who have a vested interest in the success of local schools, can be trusted to ensure that standards are kept high. Parents and employers will do everything necessary to ensure that local children succeed.

Schools (like hospitals) should be entirely independent of political interference. They should be funded and run by and for local parents. The only bureaucrat required is a secretary to assist the Head Teacher in ordering stationery supplies.

Political parties exist to maintain their power and to expand it whenever possible. No political party would even consider handing back power over schools to local communities – even though it is the right thing to do and would undoubtedly result in much better schools and much better levels of education.

Only when we get rid of political parties will we have a good educational system.

20. Hospitals and health care are better run privately.

Nothing the Government runs ever works. This is because politicians make useless managers, while the people they employ don't care enough about what they do to make any effort to do it half decently. The best (or worst) example of the failure of politicians and public employees to run anything effectively is the National Health Service (the NHS).

The NHS is a bureaucratic monster which kills more people than it saves. It is absurdly expensive, wasteful and inefficient. There are more administrators than nurses or beds. The annual cost of NHS management is an outrageous and indefensible £12.6 billion. That's double the total amount the NHS spends on accident and emergency services, dental services and maternity care. To describe the NHS as an expensive and dangerous disaster is to understate the situation. If you are taken ill the chances are that it will not be the illness that will kill you but the treatment you receive afterwards. We would, as a nation, be better off with nothing. If that sounds overstated, it isn't.

Some people are saved, of course. Road accident victims and patients requiring emergency surgery may have reason to thank the NHS for their lives. But thousands more are damaged or killed by poor prescribing, inaccurate diagnoses, dangerous vaccines, incompetent nursing and so on.

Anyone who enters an NHS hospital as a patient is putting their life at risk. If cigarette packets deserve to carry a health warning then so do hospitals.

Bevan's idea for a National Health Service was absurd. Why should the State provide a free health care service? The notion that health care should be 'free' because it is essential is rubbish. It would make more sense to say that food and water should be free.

The idea that hospitals and doctors should be part of some national system is equally nonsensical. Bigger simply means employing more bureaucrats. The existence of a central authority, and the employment of layer upon layer of administration, makes the NHS expensive and inefficient.

Britain's National Health Service is beyond repair. We need to close it down, fire all the staff (no exceptions) and start again from scratch. The NHS gives everyone an equal right to die at the hands of an uncaring and cumbersome bureaucracy. The NHS spirit died years ago. But no one has yet had the guts to bury the body – which is steadily decomposing. Most people working in the NHS admit that if they (or a member of their family) fell ill they would not want treatment in the hospital where they work. I will repeat that. Most people working in the NHS admit that if they (or a member of their family) fell ill they would not want treatment in the hospital where they work. There really isn't any need to say anything else, is there? It's a fact that merits screaming rather than comment. (The NHS used to ask staff members if they'd be happy to be treated in their hospital. It was part of their public relations propaganda. After they found that just one in four members of staff would recommend the hospital where they worked to relatives or friends, or be happy to use it themselves, the question was quietly dropped. Would you take your car to a garage knowing that three out of four mechanics who worked there wouldn't trust the garage with their own car?)

A huge rift has opened up between doctors and patients. Doctors regard patients as the enemy. And patients regard doctors with distrust.

In order to protect themselves from lawsuits doctors order batteries of investigations before daring to consider making a diagnosis. In the bad old days doctors would make diagnoses based on the patients' symptoms and their own experience and instincts. Today, diagnoses are made using tests which are far more fallible than instinct and experience.

Endless laws and regulations have separated doctors from patients. Doctors are encouraged (pressured would be a better word) to introduce appointment systems even though both patients and doctors are better off without them.

Our health care system is a failure because it is distorted by regulations, targets and legislation. Anyone who does not regard the NHS a failure should ask themselves why so many people are now flying out to India and Thailand to obtain medical care which, it is widely acknowledged, will be better and safer and much, much cheaper.

Responsibilities have been replaced by rights. And, paradoxically, the result is that in modern England many people, particularly the elderly, are denied treatment. Powerful organisations campaigning for particular groups of patients put pressure on the controlling political party and force the government to provide treatment for their group. But this is done at the expense of other patients. And so politically-correct groups (such as those requiring infertility treatment or sex change operations) are treated while the elderly (not at all politically-correct) are allowed to go blind and to die when they could be treated quite cheaply.

Things have undoubtedly also been made much worse by the European Union. It is, for example, because of the EU that general practitioners in England no longer provide 24 hour cover for their patients.

I repeat: our health care system is a failure because it is distorted by regulations, targets and legislation – some of it originating in London and much of it coming from Brussels. Replacing the NHS with a system of private medical care would employ far fewer bureaucrats but it would be infinitely fairer and better and considerably cheaper.

Don't believe me? Look at the figures.

We spend around £100 billion a year on the NHS.

There are around 60,000,000 people in the UK.

Divide 60,000,000 into £100 billion.

And you have £1,666 per head.

I could buy damned good private health cover for £1,666 a year. And so could you.

No political party would ever dare suggest closing the NHS and replacing it with a private health care system.

21. England needs an English Parliament.

Today, the United Kingdom may still (just about) be a kingdom. But it is no longer very united.

The Scots have become increasingly racist and isolationist in recent years. They have repeatedly made it clear that they hate the English. For years, calls for the break-up of the United Kingdom have come mainly from Scotland. The result is that the United Kingdom is finished.

The European Union, which wants to break up the UK and turn England into a series of colourless, administrative regions, and which has been aided in this ambition by the Scottish Parliament and the Scottish nationalists, is winning.

The Scottish and Welsh nationalists think that their countries are heading towards independence. The Scots don't realise that the Scottish parliament is, in reality, merely a regional parliament of the EU. The same is true of the Welsh parliament. The Scots and the Welsh enthusiastically support membership of the European Union because they foolishly and naively believe that staying in the EU will enable them to reach full independence.

When the European plan reaches its final stages, England will become nine anonymous regions. English history and culture will be forgotten. (The Scots and the Welsh will be allowed to retain their history and their culture as their prize for supporting the break-up of England and the UK.)

It isn't difficult to see why the authorities want to suppress England and all things English. As far as the EU is concerned the very existence of England is an embarrassment. Unlike Scotland and Wales, England is too large (and too powerful) to be a single region within the EU. Anything which promotes or defends England and Englishness is a threat and an obstacle to this aim.

Despite pressure from Scotland, the United Kingdom has been held together for several reasons.

First, the EU does not want the UK to be broken up until England has been divided into regions. If the UK breaks up while England is still a country an English Parliament will inevitably result. And, equally inevitably, English voters will vote to leave the European Union. Party politicians at Westminster do not want this to happen because the EU doesn't want it to happen.

Second, the British Parliament has for years been controlled by Scottish politicians. They want to maintain the United Kingdom because they know that their own power would disappear if the UK were broken up. Scottish-born politicians would have no place in an English Parliament. And, of course, those same Scottish politicians also know that without the huge amount of money sent north by English taxpayers, the Scottish region would be weakened. Political decisions which affect the whole country have for years been made to improve the Labour Party's chances in by-elections in Scotland.

Breaking up the United Kingdom would, in short, be disastrous for party politicians if it happened now. And so party politicians are fighting hard to protect the UK while they are fighting equally hard to destroy England and everything English.

The Scots and the Welsh are brought up to be patriotic. So are those born in Northern Ireland. But the modern English are denied the joy of patriotism and hence often grow up with no real sense of identity. When asked their nationality English people often find that 'English' is not accepted. For example, an English reader wrote to tell me that she had applied for an NHS service recently. When asked for her nationality she answered 'English'. She was told that this was not allowed. She could be Scottish, Welsh or Irish but if she was English she had to put down 'British'. Officially, England is no longer regarded as a nation and English is no longer an officially acceptable nationality. The English have been stripped of their identity, and subjected to the most ruthless variety of ethnic cleansing.

Until 2009, the post of Poet Laureate had, for nearly 400 years, been filled by eminent Englishmen. In 2009, it was announced that the new Poet Laureate would be a Scottish woman. You can't get much further from an Englishman than that.

As a result of the constant erosion of their history and culture an increasing number of English citizens are calling for the UK to be split into its component nations.

The English are becoming increasingly aware that they subsidise Scotland but that they have less power over their own lives than the Scots. Many complain that they feel as though England has been invaded by malignant Scots determined to do as much damage as they can. They are fed up with having no parliament when the Welsh, the Scots and the Northern Irish have their own parliaments. They are unhappy that the Parliament which (on behalf of the EU) rules their lives is stuffed with and controlled by Scots whereas the Scottish parliament is run by the Scots for the Scots. And they are fed up with the constant moaning and overt racist remarks from the Scots. Many Englishmen and women are angered that whereas Scottish (and Welsh) nationalists tend to be regarded as proud patriots, English nationalists are dismissed as racists and bigots.

There is great resentment in England at the way that English taxpayers are increasingly being expected to subsidise the Scots. How fast will resentment build among English students as they struggle to pay off the huge debts they have incurred as a result of the Government's student loan scheme? And how much is that resentment going to be fuelled by the knowledge that students from Scotland, who have studied alongside them at English universities, can start life with no debts whatsoever because their bills have been paid by English taxpayers? How fast will resentment build when the English realise just how free the Scottish 'government' has been with English money. Lowly State functionaries in Scotland are paid more than responsible professionals in the rest of the UK. State spending in Scotland is now at 54.7% of GDP. That is the highest in the world and 20% higher per capita than in England, which is funding the Scottish 'government's generosity. (English taxpayers pay £1.32 a year each for the Scottish parliament's operating expenses.)

The English are conscious, too, that greedy Scottish financial institutions are largely to blame for the financial crisis in England.

Much resentment built up in England when two large Scottish banks (RBS and HBOS) failed and were bailed out by English taxpayers. English investors and employees paid the price yet again for Scottish incompetence.

By early 2009, many English folk wanted Scotland to leave the UK.

There is also growing resentment at the fact that many leading politicians in the House of Commons (including the last two Prime Ministers) are Scottish. The fact that the Scottish dominated Labour Party has done enormous damage to the economy, and that English taxpayers are now being expected to pay for the damage that has been done, has not gone unnoticed.

Moreover, the English are aware that although the now inevitable break-up of the United Kingdom will be disastrous for Scotland and Wales it will be excellent news for England and the English.

In recent years there has been a clear rise in English nationalism. There is a widespread belief that England would be stronger, richer and happier as a separate nation.

Many English citizens want Hadrian's Wall rebuilt and proper boundaries erected so that if Scots want to come south they must obtain a visa and then go home when their holiday or business trip is over. (Some would like to see Offa's Dyke reconstituted too.)

England's only hope is to create an English Parliament, escape from the European Union and declare independence. This is a rearguard action and it's one that everyone who cares about England should fight. Those who represent England in the English Parliament must have been born in England. England must be administered by Englishmen and Englishwomen.

As long as governments are formed by political parties there will be no English Parliament. England will only survive with a parliament of independents.

22. We need a Ministry of Defence, not a Ministry of War.

England clearly needs an army, a navy and an airforce with which to defend itself against aggressors. And these must be supplied, and paid for, by the nation.

But we should only give politicians the authority to fight wars when we have been attacked. The Ministry of Defence is, after all, the Ministry of Defence and not the Ministry of War or the Ministry of Attack.

Those who oppose foreign interventions are likely to be dismissed as isolationists. This is nonsense, of course. The real isolationists are the ones who bomb and kill innocent people, and who impose sanctions and embargoes on selected countries (which result in the deaths of innocent babies and children) because they disagree with the nation's policies or want their oil, but who nevertheless fund tyrants and dictators whose views happen to fit with the views of our leaders.

Nineteenth Century statesman Richard Cobden opposed all foreign interventions by the English Government. He wasn't regarded as an isolationist. He was known as the International Man.

23. We should abandon the Welfare State, and the benefits system.

The Welfare State, whereby vast amounts of money are doled out to virtually anyone who asks for it, has damaged everyone. It has damaged those who receive the money because it has taken away their sense of independence and, very often, their willingness to work and look after themselves. And it has damaged the rest of our community because it has taken away our sense of community as well as our sense of responsibility. Instead of giving money to help the genuinely poor we feel resentful about being forced to help people whose needs may not be genuine.

We have been brainwashed into thinking that the State must take responsibility for everything. But this has happened simply because those who work for the State want to control everything; they want to extend their power into every aspect of our lives.

Thousands of people are on benefits simply because they are, they claim, too fat to work. Thousands more walked away from jobs (or offers of employment) because the after-tax salary they were offered would result in them being poorer than if they stayed on benefits. The concept of responsibility has been replaced by the idea of rights. Every time the Government offers more money to people who live on benefits it increases the incentive for millions to avoid work.

Much of the money devoted to welfare is spent on bureaucracy, and government welfare programmes are easily abused by the givers and the receivers. The end result is that the money handed out does more harm than good; the people handing the stuff out become hardened, the people receiving it resent the way they are treated and the whole process encourages universal despair, endemic laziness and long-term dependence on the State. (The people handing out the money become just as dependent on the State as the people receiving it. And their value to the State is no greater.)

In the 1970s I suggested that placing dustbins full of money on street corners would be cheaper and just as fair as the system of welfare payments to which so many had become accustomed. Today the dustbins would need to be replaced by skips, but the principle remains the same.

I am a fiscal conservative but a social liberal. I believe in looking after people and providing services but in making sure that the money is well spent.

And there is a much simpler, easier, fairer and cheaper way of eradicating poverty and ridding our streets of beggars. Here it is.

Everyone over 16 should get a basic tax-free living allowance of £10,000 a year (rising each year according to inflation). And that's it. Nothing else. The allowance should last for life. In or out of work you get the basic living allowance. If you want more than that you have to earn it.

The cost of this annual allowance would be more than covered by the cost of cutting out the cost of the benefits payments and the bureaucrats who are employed to service the system. Providing a basic fixed income will mean that there will be no need for unemployment benefit or sickness benefit. Nor will there be any need for the nation to pay old age pensions. The nation will save a fortune in administration.

So, in the new England, the State will pay us all a citizen's basic income. The State will pay us instead of us paying income tax. This would free everyone from exploitation, eradicate the need for unemployment or welfare benefits, eradicate poverty, end involuntary prostitution, do much to reduce crime levels and encourage people to work (in order to increase their income). The citizen's basic income would stop people feeling resentment about their neighbours who don't work. And it would allow the Government to find more productive employment for the vast army of bureaucrats involved in administrating the huge variety of State benefits. The saving to the nation would be phenomenal. Millions of man-hours would be freed for more creative enterprises.

Social security payments currently cost the nation around £200 billion a year. Paying the bureaucrats and administering the payments costs half as much again. With ten million pensioners, the State pension scheme costs at least another £50 billion (and the numbers are rising fast). Administering the pension scheme costs billions more. Pensions and other payments to former public sector workers cost billions.

My idea of giving every man and woman in the country a lifetime income of £10,000 a year would be cheaper than our current State pension and benefits programme. And it would be simpler and fairer and better both for individuals and for the State.

No political party would ever have the courage, or the imagination, to introduce such a scheme.

24. Interest rates should be allowed to fluctuate according to the market place.

Why should a government of buffoons (or a set of half-witted civil servants or bankers) be allowed to decide what interest rates will be? Bankers, bureaucrats and politicians have proved that they are incapable of looking after the economy. Let the economy look after itself. The price of capital in a capitalist society is too important to be left to politicians and bureaucrats. Interest rates should be free floating.

Finally...

There are many things we could and should do to improve our world; many things we could do if we had a Parliament of independent MPs, freed from the constraints of a political party.

During the banking crisis of 2008 we might have been able to get through the depression more speedily if, instead of giving billions to the bankers (to spend on parties and bonuses) the Government had given £1,000,000 tax free to everyone over the age of 50.

The two sole stipulations would have been, first, that they retired from work and did not reapply for employment and, second, that they should buy two things with their windfall: a new house worth less than £250,000 (to live in or to let) and a new, English-made car worth at least £5,000.

This would have sorted the car industry. And it would have got the housing market moving. It would have also provided several million jobs and, therefore, solved the unemployment problem. It would have meant more income (and therefore more spending money) for all the 30-somethings and 40-somethings who were promoted.

And it would have cost far less than bailing out the bankrupt banks and greedy bankers who had helped create the financial crisis in the first place.

Outlandish? Certainly. Would it have worked? Possibly. Would the political parties, with their own agendas, have even considered such a plan? Of course not.

Without a political party running our lives (and other political parties trying to snatch power from them) we would be free to consider all sorts of solutions, and to look critically at other aspects of our lives – aspects which the political parties never even question.

So, for example, we rear animals for food in barbaric, unnatural conditions. We fill the animals with antibiotics, growth hormones and countless other chemicals and then we kill them in circumstances which would shame anyone with a conscience. The animals die in a burst of adrenalin. The meat we eat contains carcinogens and far too much fat to be healthy. It's hardly surprising that meat eaters suffer far more from cancer than vegetarians.

We allow farmers to spray known carcinogens onto our fields. We allow our water supplies to be polluted. We allow large international companies to sell genetically modified plants and we allow scientists to play around with genetically engineered animals. We even allow them to mix human and animal genes in experiments to create hybrid creatures which we can use as slaves, organ donors or food.

None of this is sensible, safe or morally acceptable.

There are so many other things we accept as 'normal' which should be looked at critically.

Why do we use money raised from taxes to support sportsmen and artists? These aren't things the State should be funding.

Why are we forced (by law) to pay an annual fee to the BBC? Why must we support a profligate and biased organisation which is steadily destroying freedom of speech in England? If the BBC can persuade people to pay subscriptions for its services then let it survive. If it cannot, then let it die.

Despite the fact that we have, for years, been fighting a 'war on drugs' England has a booming drug addiction problem. The number of addicts grows constantly. The reason is easy to see. Spending vast amounts of money on addicts has 'victimised' and popularised addiction and turned it into a profitable activity. In reality, heroin and cocaine are not particularly addictive drugs (it is far harder to get off benzodiazepine tranquillisers, for example) and the nation's expensive drug addiction problem could have been dealt with far more effectively if politicians had put more effort into arresting and imprisoning those selling drugs. (And a little more effort should have been put into helping the real victims of drug addiction – those innocent members of the public who are robbed by addicts looking for money with which to buy drugs.)

By giving money and homes to single, young girls who get pregnant politicians have encouraged the increase in the incidence of teenage pregnancies. They may have ensured a core of voting support for their party, but they have also ensured that the problem continues to grow.

Our political parties say and do nothing about these things because it is in their interests to keep quiet. Political parties don't care about people. Like large, international corporations they care only about their own survival.

There are some huge problems ahead. And the world is going to change in many, many fundamental ways.

The Arabs will not be so rich when the oil runs out. China is on the rise. The Chinese are busy buying up gold so that they can turn their currency, the yuan, into the world's new reserve currency. When they're ready for that then the dollar will go into a rapid and terminal decline, America will be finished and the Chinese will rule the world. China and India are the future of capitalism. America, a nation with which our politicians routinely claim to have a 'special relationship' has no strengths, no money, no other friends and no future. Obama will prove to be the biggest disappointment in politics for generations.

We will need powerful and far thinking leaders to cope with these changes. We will need leaders with intelligence, vision, insight, intuition, imagination and integrity to lead us into and through the dark days, weeks, months, years and decades ahead.

And with a Parliament consisting of independent men and women there is a much greater chance that those who manage our country will be capable of a little lateral thinking.

Only an independent Parliament, controlled by strong, independent individuals would even discuss the ideas I've suggested in this book.

Political parties deal with crises with their own interests at heart, and always manipulate situations to suit their own political advantage. Political parties are a dangerous luxury we can no longer afford.

Without a Parliament controlled by political parties the future is invigorating, exciting and full of hope.

The message is clear and unavoidable.

The Author

Vernon Coleman was an angry young man for as long as it was decently possible. He then turned into an angry middle-aged man. And now, with no effort whatsoever, he has matured into being an angry old man. He is, he confesses, just as angry as he ever was. Indeed, he may be even angrier because, he says, the more he learns about life the more things he finds to be angry about.

Cruelty, prejudice and injustice are the three things most likely to arouse his well-developed sense of ire but he admits that, at a pinch, inefficiency, incompetence and greed will do almost as well. He does not cope well with bossy people, particularly when they are dressed in uniform and attempting to confiscate his Swiss Army penknife. 'Being told I can't do something has always seemed to me sufficient reason to do it,' he says. 'And being told that I must do something has always seemed to me a very good reason not to do it.'

The author has a pathological contempt for pomposity, hypocrisy and the sort of unthinking political correctness which attracts support from *Guardian* reading pseudo-intellectuals. He also has a passionate loathing for those in authority who do not understand that unless their authority is tempered with compassion and a sense of responsibility the end result must always be an extremely unpleasant brand of totalitarianism.

This is his last book on politics. He says he believes that this book (*Bloodless Revolution*) contains the best answer he can provide and there seems little point in continuing to redefine the problem when he has already defined the answer to the best of his ability.

Vernon Coleman has written for *The Guardian, Daily Telegraph, Sunday Telegraph, Observer, Sunday Times, Daily Mail, Mail on Sunday, Daily Express, Sunday Express, Daily Star, The Sun, News of the World, Daily Mirror, Sunday Mirror, The People, Woman, Woman's Own, Spectator, Punch, The Lady* and hundreds of other leading publications in Britain and around the world. His books have been published by Pan, Penguin, Corgi, Arrow and many other publishers in the UK, and reproduced by scores of discerning publishers around the world.

He has never had a proper job (in the sense of working for someone else in regular, paid employment, with a cheque or pay packet at the end of the week or month) but he has had freelance and temporary employment in many forms. He has, for example, had paid employment as: magician's assistant, postman, fish delivery van driver, production line worker, chemical laboratory assistant, author, publisher, draughtsman, meals on wheels driver, feature writer, drama critic, book reviewer, columnist, surgeon, police surgeon, industrial medical officer, social worker, night club operator, property developer, magazine editor, general practitioner, private doctor, television presenter, radio presenter, agony aunt, university lecturer, casualty doctor and care home assistant. He is still a fully registered medical practitioner and licensed G.P.

He doesn't like yappy dogs, big snarly dogs with saliva dripping from their fangs or people who think that wearing a uniform automatically gives them status and rights. He likes trains, dislikes planes and used to like cars until idiots invented speed cameras, bus lanes and car parks where the spaces are so narrow that only the slimmest, and tinniest of vehicles will fit in.

He is fond of cats, pens and notebooks and used to like watching cricket until the authorities sold out and allowed people to paint slogans on the grass. His interests and hobbies include animals, books, photography, drawing, chess, backgammon, cinema, philately, billiards, sitting in cafes and on benches and collecting Napoleana. He likes log fires and bonfires, motor racing and music by Mahler and dislikes politicians, bureaucrats and cauliflower cheese. He likes videos but loathes DVDs. His favourite people in history include Napoleon Bonaparte, W.G.Grace, William

Cobbett, P.G.Wodehouse, Jerome K. Jerome, and Walter Raleigh all of whom had more than it takes and most of whom were English. (Napoleon would have been if he'd had the chance.)

He lives in the village of Bilbury in Devon and enjoys malt whisky, toasted muffins and old films. He is married to and devoted to Donna Antoinette who is the kindest, sweetest, most sensitive woman a man could hope to meet and who, as an undeserved but welcome bonus, makes the very best roast parsnips on the planet. Their ambition is to run a small butterfly farm together in Bilbury.

For a catalogue of Vernon Coleman's books please write to:

Publishing House
Trinity Place
Barnstaple
Devon EX32 9HG
England

Telephone   01271 328892
Fax   01271 328768

Outside the UK:
Telephone   +44 1271 328892
Fax   +44 1271 328768

Or visit our website:
www.vernoncoleman.com

The Bloodless Revolution
How we can change the world in one day

To order a single copy of this book send a cheque or postal order for £4.99 payable to 'Publishing House' to the address below. Or order online at www.vernoncoleman.com. Copies are also available from all good bookshops.

Bulk copies are available (direct from the publishers only) at special prices for distribution to friends, relatives and journalists.

5 copies	£15	10 copies	£20
20 copies	£30	50 copies	£50
100 copies	£80	500 copies	£350

All these prices include p&p in the UK (for overseas orders please contact us for carriage details)

Bulk copies are available only by cheque or postal order, and by writing to: Publishing House, Trinity Place, Barnstaple, Devon EX32 9HG.

Remember to enclose your name and address for delivery (along with your cheque/PO payable to Publishing House). Remember: you cannot order at these special prices either on-line or from other bookshops.

> ## "Revolutions are only impossible before they take place. Afterwards they were inevitable"
> ### VERNON COLEMAN

Published in paperback by Blue Books, 192 pages price £4.99
Publishing House • Trinity Place • Barnstaple • Devon EX32 9HG •
England Telephone 01271 328892 • Fax 01271 328768
www.vernoncoleman.com

Other books by Vernon Coleman

Gordon Is A Moron

In *Gordon is a Moron* I've explained how Brown's stupidity and incompetence have weakened Britain for generations to come.

If you share my horror at the lowering of quality and standards in public life you will, I suspect, also share my belief that no one exemplifies the lowering more dramatically than Gordon the Moron. I have tried to deal with Brown in an objective and academic way but I make no apologies if any of my contempt has seeped into my prose. What have we done to deserve public servants such as Brown? It must have been something pretty terrible.

taken from the Preface of *Gordon is a Moron*

"Thank you, thank you. An amazing book. Skillfully written, entertaining, frightening and long overdue." (A.J by e-mail)

"Brilliantly perceptive biography." (J.W. Northants)

"If you want to know the damage that the Moron has done to the economy of Britain, this is the book you should read. A page turner filled with factually backed accusations. The effect of Brown's actions on the finances of his country, its institutions and its Constitution are all examined and picked apart." (P.H. Amazon review)

"Thank you for writing *Gordon is a Moron*. I have just packed one for David Cameron and one for William Hague. I have also advised them that this book should be sent to every college and school and to all authorities." (S. P. J., Wales)

"Why, you will ask, has no one in the media charted the cataclysmic damage caused by this dour control freak in a way that makes clear what has happened? You won't get it on the state sympathetic BBC, and you won't hear it talked about in the Westminster Village. None of the matters discussed can be genuinely rebutted because they are all true. Read it and weep." (R.B. Amazon review)

Published in paperback by Blue Books, 160 pages price £9.99
Order from Publishing House • Trinity Place • Barnstaple • Devon
EX32 9HG • England Telephone 01271 328892 • Fax 01271 328768
www.vernoncoleman.com

Other books by Vernon Coleman

What Happens Next?

Gordon Brown and the Labour Party have led us into a depression, turned us into a fascist country and made Britain the weakest nation in the developed world.

We live in troubled and confusing times. These are the times no one wants to live through; the times that no one ever thought would arrive. But without doubt they look set to continue for a very long time indeed.

No country has ever fallen so quickly and so far. In just over a decade Britain has become a laughing stock; a pathetic, tramp of a country, ashamed of its past, ashamed of its heroes, ashamed of its achievements, ashamed of its greatness. Britain has been destroyed by the politically correct and the multi-culturalists; by the greedy and the uncaring.

What Happens Next? is a look at the future. But as you read it you will, I suspect, find yourself drawing the same conclusions that I have drawn. The current financial crisis will segue directly into the peak oil crisis. Surviving the future will require an ability to understand what is happening and to predict at least some of the possible consequences.

In chapter after chapter I've lain down the evidence in a simple and straightforward way, and tried to explain what you can do to protect yourself and your family.

Vernon Coleman

Published in paperback by Blue Books, 347 pages price £15.99
Order from Publishing House • Trinity Place • Barnstaple • Devon
EX32 9HG • England Telephone 01271 328892 • Fax 01271 328768
www.vernoncoleman.com

How To Protect And Preserve Your Freedom, Identity And Privacy

Thousands of people fall victim to identity theft every year. The consequences can be devastating and can take years to sort out.

Banks and Government departments take poor care of the vital, private information they demand. It's hardly surprising that identity theft is the fastest growing crime in the world.

Amazingly, there are scores of ways that your identity can be stolen. The majority of people aren't aware of just how vulnerable they are until it's too late.

How To Protect And Preserve Your Freedom, Identity And Privacy gives advice on:

- What to do if you're a victim of identity theft.
- The type of phone that can protect you against fraud.
- The tricks fraudsters use at cash machines.
- The signs which show that your identity may have been stolen.
- What you should watch out for when using your credit card in shops and restaurants.
- How you can protect your security before you go on holiday.
- Why you should be wary of the 'postman' knocking at your door – and the e-mails you should be frightened of.
- How answering your phone could leave you vulnerable to fraud.
- Why you should be wary about the clothes you wear.
- Why just leaving your Internet lead plugged in could leave you open to fraud... and much, much more.

Vernon Coleman's best-seller contains crucial security tips for personal survival in the 21st century.

Published in paperback by Blue Books, 128 pages price £9.99
Order from Publishing House • Trinity Place • Barnstaple • Devon
EX32 9HG • England Telephone 01271 328892 • Fax 01271 328768
www.vernoncoleman.com

Other books by Vernon Coleman

Oil Apocalypse

How to Survive, Protect Your Family And Profit Through The Coming Years of Crisis

Why the oil apocalypse is inevitable. How and why our dependence on oil will end in tears. And how you can prepare yourself and your family. Also includes

- Our unhealthy addiction to a gift of nature
- Peak oil: the beginning of the end of civilisation
- What will happen when the oil runs out
- Your personal survival plan
- Investing to survive the oil apocalypse

'I am writing to offer my sincere congratulations on such a well researched book. It made fascinating reading and personally I accept your frightening prognosis...I write as one who...spent several years working in the...oil and gas industry.' (R.W. SUSSEX)

'Congratulations on this book. Full of indisputable facts and common sense.' (P.R., LONDON)

'...once again you are ahead of the pack!' (D.K., EXETER)
'...the most disturbing and enlightening book I have ever read. No book has ever had such a profound effect on me.' (M.C., SHEFFIELD)

'Intense reading. Coleman's message is blunt and this book will frighten you, but bury your head in the sand at your own peril. If you don't believe him then keep an eye on the price at the pump.'
(FIVE STAR BOOK, GEOFFREY TAYLOR, SHROPSHIRE STAR)

"Generally I don't subscribe to doom mongers books. But I read *Oil Apocalypse* this weekend and it was terrific. Very insightful. Brilliant book. Five stars." (J.S., BY E-MAIL)

Published in paperback by Blue Books, 160 pages price £12.99
Order from Publishing House • Trinity Place • Barnstaple • Devon
EX32 9HG • England Telephone 01271 328892 • Fax 01271 328768
www.vernoncoleman.com

Other books by Vernon Coleman

The O.F.P.I.S. File

"The Most Powerful And Revealing Book About The EU Ever Published"

- Were we taken into the EU illegally?
- Fraud, the EU and our money
- The EU's regionalisation of Britain
- ID cards and your disappearing freedom
- The EU's policy on immigration: a ticking time bomb
- The EU and the stupidity of the biofuels directive
- The Lisbon Treaty, the EU Constitution, the Queen, a good many lies and the end of Britain
- Why the EU is just like the old USSR
- Why English (and British) history is being suppressed
- The case for leaving the EU: why England should declare independence

"Had to thank you and praise you for your incredible work getting out your informative book on the EU." (M.W., WALES)

"I have just finished reading *The OFPIS File* and think it probably the best yet, not only because it lights up the EU scam in a way that few can, but has such a great deal of relevant detail." (J.M., LANCS)

"Thank you for sending me your *OFPIS* book which I managed to read in two days flat. Your books are very readable and are hard to put down once started." (A.K., MIDDLESEX)

"Vernon Coleman is well regarded in our circles as the author of several fine books exposing the machinations of the Europhile elite, and for others in which he emerges as a sincere and thoughtful English patriot. He most definitely is neither a crank nor an alarmist." IDENTITY MAGAZINE

Published in paperback by Blue Books, 334 pages price £15.99
Order from Publishing House • Trinity Place • Barnstaple • Devon
EX32 9HG • England Telephone 01271 328892 • Fax 01271 328768
www.vernoncoleman.com